ASSESSING LEARNING

in the

STANDARDS-BASED CLASSROOM

A Practical Guide for Teachers

JAN K. HOEGH

JEFF FLYGARE

TAMMY HEFLEBOWER

PHILIP B. WARRICK

MARZANO
Resources

555 North Morton Street
Bloomington, IN 47404
888.849.0851
FAX: 866.801.1447

email: info@MarzanoResources.com
MarzanoResources.com

Visit **MarzanoResources.com/reproducibles** to download the free reproducibles in this book.

Printed in the United States of America

Library of Congress Cataloging-in-Publication Data

Names: Hoegh, Jan K., author. | Flygare, Jeff, author. | Heflebower, Tammy,
   author. | Warrick, Philip B., author.
Title: Assessing learning in the standards-based classroom : a practical
   guide for teachers / Jan K. Hoegh, Jeff Flygare, Tammy Heflebower,
   Philip B. Warrick.
Description: Bloomington, IN : Marzano Resources, [2022] | Includes
   bibliographical references and index.
Identifiers: LCCN 2022031742 (print) | LCCN 2022031743 (ebook) | ISBN
   9781943360741 (Paperback) | ISBN 9781943360758 (eBook)
Subjects: LCSH: Education--Standards--United States. | Grading and marking
   (Students)--United States. | Educational tests and
   measurements--Interpretation. | Students--Rating of--United States.
Classification: LCC LB3060.83 .H64 2022 (print) | LCC LB3060.83 (ebook) |
   DDC 379.1/580973--dc23/eng/20221028
LC record available at https://lccn.loc.gov/2022031742
LC ebook record available at https://lccn.loc.gov/2022031743

Production Team
President and Publisher: Douglas M. Rife
Associate Publisher: Sarah Payne-Mills
Managing Production Editor: Kendra Slayton
Editorial Director: Todd Brakke
Art Director: Rian Anderson
Copy Chief: Jessi Finn
Senior Production Editor: Laurel Hecker
Content Development Specialist: Amy Rubenstein
Copy Editor: Mark Hain
Proofreader: Charlotte Jones
Text and Cover Designer: Laura Cox
Associate Editor: Sarah Ludwig
Editorial Assistants: Charlotte Jones and Elijah Oates

Acknowledgments

Thank you to all the educators, schools, and districts that gave us permission to include their products and processes in this resource. Your willingness to share is a means of supporting educators everywhere and we are grateful!

Marzano Resources would like to thank the following reviewers:

Courtney Burdick
Apprenticeship Mentor Teacher
Fort Smith Public Schools
Fort Smith, Arkansas

Jenna Fanshier
Sixth-Grade Teacher
Hesston Middle School
Hesston, Kansas

Rachel Swearengin
Fifth-Grade Teacher
Manchester Park Elementary School
Olathe, Kansas

Emily Terry
English Teacher
Kinard Core Knowledge Middle School
Fort Collins, Colorado

Sheryl Walters
Instructional Design Lead
Calgary Academy
Calgary, Alberta

Table of Contents

Reproducibles are in italics

About the Authors

Jan K. Hoegh has been an educator for over thirty-five years and an author and associate for Marzano Resources since 2010. Prior to joining the Marzano team, she was a classroom teacher, building leader, professional development specialist, high school assistant principal, curriculum coordinator, and assistant director of statewide assessment for the Nebraska Department of Education, where her primary focus was Nebraska State Accountability test development. Jan has served on a variety of statewide and national standards and assessment committees and has presented at numerous conferences around the world.

As an associate with Marzano Resources, Jan works with educators across the United States and beyond as they strive to improve student achievement. Her passion for education, combined with extensive knowledge of curriculum, instruction, and assessment, provide credible support for teachers, leaders, schools, and districts. High-quality classroom assessment and grading practices are her primary training focuses. She is the author of *A Handbook for Developing and Using Proficiency Scales in the Classroom* and coauthor of *Collaborative Teams That Transform Schools*, *A School Leader's Guide to Standards-Based Grading*, *A Teacher's Guide to Standards-Based Learning*, and *Planning and Teaching in the Standards-Based Classroom*, as well as other publications.

Jan holds a bachelor of arts degree in elementary education and a master of arts in educational administration, both from the University of Nebraska at Kearney. She also earned a specialization in assessment from the University of Nebraska–Lincoln.

Jeff Flygare is a former classroom teacher, English department chair, professional developer, and building leader. During his twenty-six-year career teaching middle school drama and high school English in Academy District 20 in El Paso County, Colorado, he taught nearly every course in his school's English department. Jeff developed classes in mythology, Shakespeare, philosophy, and comparative religions, and worked with social studies colleagues to create an interdisciplinary class called World Studies, which he team-taught successfully for seventeen years. He taught Advanced Placement (AP) English classes for twenty-one years and served as an AP English literature reader and table leader for Educational Testing Service for many years. He adopted standards-based learning in his classroom and successfully taught students at all levels in a standards-based environment for many years.

Jeff also has a strong theatrical background, working first as an actor and then as a director at a major regional theater company in Colorado. He directed many high school productions, both traditional and Shakespearean, as well. As a Marzano Resources associate, Jeff travels around the world to work with educators on topics involving curriculum, instruction, and assessment. He is the author of *Close Reading in the Secondary Classroom*, coauthor of *A Teacher's Guide to Standards-Based Learning*, and lead author of *Planning and Teaching in the Standards-Based Classroom*.

Jeff holds a bachelor's degree in English from the State University of New York at Buffalo, a master's degree in English from the University of Colorado Denver, and a master's degree in education with an endorsement in gifted education from the University of Colorado Colorado Springs.

Tammy Heflebower, EdD, is a highly sought-after school leader and consultant with vast experience in urban, rural, and suburban districts throughout the United States, Australia, Canada, Denmark, Great Britain, and the Netherlands. She has served as an award-winning classroom teacher, building leader, district leader, regional professional development director, and national and international trainer. She has also been an adjunct professor of curriculum, instruction, and assessment at several universities and a prominent member and leader of numerous statewide and national educational organizations.

Tammy was vice president and then senior scholar at Marzano Resources and continues to work as an author and associate with Marzano Resources and Solution Tree. In addition, she is the CEO of her own company, !nspire Inc.: Education and Business Solutions, specializing in powerful presentation and facilitation techniques, which she writes about and shares worldwide. Tammy is sole author of the *Presenting Perfected* book series and lead author of *Crafting Your Message*: *An Educator's Guide to Perfect Presentations*. She is also lead author of the best-selling, award-winning *A School Leader's Guide to Standards-Based Grading*, lead author of the award finalist *A Teacher's Guide to Standards-Based Learning*, and coauthor of *Collaborative Teams That Transform Schools*: *The Next Step in PLCs* and *Teaching and Assessing 21st Century Skills*. She is a contributing author to over a dozen other books and publications, many of which have been translated into multiple languages and are referenced internationally.

Tammy holds a bachelor of arts degree from Hastings College in Hastings, Nebraska, where she was honored as Outstanding Young Alumna and her volleyball team was inducted into the athletic hall of fame. She has a master of arts from the University of Nebraska Omaha and she received her educational administrative endorsement and doctorate from the University of Nebraska–Lincoln.

 **Philip B. Warrick, EdD,** spent the first twenty-five years of his education career as a teacher, assistant principal, principal, and superintendent and has experience leading schools in the states of Nebraska and Texas. He was named 1998 Nebraska Outstanding New Principal of the Year and was the 2005 Nebraska State High School Principal of the Year. In 2003, he was one of the initial participants in the Nebraska Educational Leadership Institute, conducted by the Gallup Corporation at Gallup University in Omaha. In 2008, Phil was hired as the campus principal at Round Rock High School in Round Rock, Texas. In 2010, he was invited to be an inaugural participant in the Texas Principals' Visioning Institute, where he collaborated with other principals from the state to develop a vision for effective practices in Texas schools. In 2011, Phil joined the Solution Tree–Marzano Resources team and works as an author and global consultant in the areas of High Reliability School leadership, instruction and instructional coaching, assessment, grading, and collaborative teaming.

Phil earned a bachelor of science from Chadron State College in Chadron, Nebraska, and his master's and doctoral degrees from the University of Nebraska–Lincoln.

To book Jan K. Hoegh, Jeff Flygare, Tammy Heflebower, or Philip B. Warrick for professional development, contact pd@MarzanoResources.com.

Introduction

Assessment has always been a prominent component of education. However, its role is changing. Traditionally, the purpose of assessment was to assign grades at the ends of courses or units, measure supposed aptitude for higher education, and compare students to each other (Marzano, Dodson, Simms, & Wipf, 2022). As the field of education shifts its goals toward ensuring all students learn, the purpose of assessment becomes more integrated with instruction. Assessment provides information about what students know and can do, what they still need to learn, and how the teacher should adjust instruction to help students meet the goals of the lesson, unit, or course.

In alignment with this more expansive view of assessment, education expert Robert J. Marzano (2010) provided a practitioner-friendly definition for classroom assessment: "anything a teacher does to gather information about a student's knowledge or skill regarding a specific topic" (p. 22). Professors of education Christopher R. Gareis and Leslie W. Grant (2015) agreed, saying,

> The way teachers see student learning is through a process known as assessment; and assessment, like teaching, is integrally related to our definition of learning. We define assessment as the process of using methods or tools to collect information about student learning. (p. 2)

In order to enact this conception of assessment, teachers must provide assessment opportunities and then engage in careful analysis of the results for the sake of planning or adjusting instruction. And it is clear that this approach is becoming more common. According to the National Council on Teacher Quality, "Teachers increasingly find themselves not just working in isolation to divine the instructional implications of assessment results, but also working collaboratively with colleagues to use results to improve the performance of individuals, classes, grades or the entire school" (Greenberg & Walsh, 2012, p. 2).

If educators are to use assessment data to improve results, those data must be based on high-quality assessments and assessment practices. This is the primary goal of this book: to support classroom teachers with relevant and necessary information about classroom assessment that produces timely and accurate information about student learning that teachers can use for instructional purposes. However, the view of assessment as integrated with learning requires a holistic, systemic approach. The methods we recommend in this book function as a component of *standards-based learning*.

An Overview of Standards-Based Learning

A focus on standards has been a requirement for educators since the mid to late 1990s. Schools and districts are committed to ensuring that students demonstrate mastery of the intended knowledge provided by state departments of education. While there are various plausible approaches to standards-based learning, we propose that there are certain critical components within this endeavor, including priority standards, proficiency scales, and instructional cycles that include high-quality assessments. When schools or districts address these components, educators engage in what we term *standards-based learning*.

Priority Standards

In the standards-based classroom, a set of priority standards identifies the essential content, including both knowledge and skills, which constitutes the majority of the curriculum for a particular course or content area and grade level. Teachers simply do not have sufficient instructional time during the K–12 span to provide instruction on all state standards as written, and students do not have enough time to learn them (Hoegh, 2020; Marzano, 2003). If teachers do not narrow the curriculum to a set of essential priorities, they find themselves moving rapidly through an enormous amount of content, never having the time to ensure student proficiency on the required standards. Prioritizing the curriculum has the effect of providing enough instructional time to allow teachers to go deep on the essentials.

Prioritization of standards should be a schoolwide or districtwide process, guided by criteria like endurance, leverage, readiness, teacher judgment, and appearance on high-stakes assessments (Ainsworth, 2003; Heflebower, Hoegh, & Warrick, 2014). Because priority standards identify the essentials of the curriculum for a content area, grade level, or course, and because instructional time is limited, the number of priority standards should be relatively small. In our experience, it is common for a teacher or team of teachers to identify ten to fifteen priority standards for a single content area and grade level or course. This number is a suggestion and not a universally applied rule; for some grade levels and content areas, the total number of priority standards may be fewer, and sometimes the number is greater. The key idea to remember is that by keeping the number of priority standards low, the likelihood is greater that teachers will have the instructional time they need to ensure that students are proficient on these very important standards.

Note that no standards go untaught. Standards not deemed priority are categorized as supporting or supplemental, not discarded. All standards are addressed in instruction, but the majority of the instructional time and assessment focus will be on priority standards. The priority standards will constitute the bulk of instruction and they will, in general terms, form the basis of assessment, feedback, grading, and reporting.

For additional information on the process of identifying priority and supporting standards, we refer readers to *A School Leader's Guide to Standards-Based Grading* (Heflebower et al., 2014) and *Leading Standards-Based Learning* (Heflebower, Hoegh, & Warrick, 2021).

Proficiency Scales

Once teachers have identified the priority standards, they need a way of measuring student progress toward proficiency on these standards. This is one of the purposes of a proficiency scale. A proficiency scale identifies performance at different levels relative to a standard, either a priority standard or an associated learning goal. Additionally, a proficiency scale identifies learning targets at each level of the scale, and thus the proficiency scale serves as a useful map of students' learning progression to proficiency in the overall learning goal (Hoegh, 2020; Marzano, 2010; Marzano & Kendall, 1996). Figure I.1 displays a sample proficiency scale.

Score 4.0	The student will solve an engineering problem involving decisions about which material, based on its properties, will best satisfy a set of requirements and constraints.
Score 3.5	In addition to score 3.0 performance, partial success at score 4.0 content
Score 3.0	The student will classify materials based on their properties (magnetism, conductivity, density, solubility, boiling point, melting point).
Score 2.5	No major errors or omissions regarding score 2.0 content, and partial success at score 3.0 content
Score 2.0	The student will recognize and recall basic vocabulary, such as *boiling point*, *conductivity*, *density*, *magnetism*, *melting point*, and *solubility*. Students will perform basic processes, such as: • Making observations to identify the properties of a material • Taking measurements to identify the properties of a material
Score 1.5	Partial success at score 2.0 content, and major errors or omissions regarding score 3.0 content
Score 1.0	With help, the student will achieve partial success at score 2.0 content but not at score 3.0 content
Score 0.5	With help, partial success at score 2.0 content but not at score 3.0 content
Score 0.0	Even with help, the student has no success

Source: Marzano, Norford, Finn, & Finn, 2017, p. 29.

Figure I.1: Sample proficiency scale for material properties, grade 5 science.

The proficiency scale identifies the standard or learning goal at score 3.0, simpler content related to the standard at score 2.0, and advanced content at score 4.0. All students are expected to master the score 3.0 content. It is useful to think in terms of a proficiency scale for each identified priority standard, although it can sometimes be true that a single priority standard may be complex and multifaceted enough to require more than a single scale. It is also possible for multiple standards to be represented on a single proficiency scale if they are narrowly focused and closely related.

In this example scale, the score 3.0 learning target, "The student will classify materials based on their properties (magnetism, conductivity, density, solubility, boiling point, melting point)," specifically identifies a skill that students will perform. Implied within that learning target is a set of factual knowledge that will be essential for students to perform the processes. Students will need to know the differences between magnetism, conductivity, density, solubility, boiling point, and melting point. Further, they will need to know more basic forms of the process described in the score 3.0 learning target. This basic knowledge and these simpler forms of the process are identified in the learning targets at score 2.0. In a high-quality proficiency scale, the learning targets at score 2.0 have a direct relationship with the score 3.0 learning targets. Mastery of the score 2.0 learning targets typically occurs before the teacher asks a student to master the learning targets at score 3.0. As a result, the levels of a proficiency scale inform the sequence of instruction.

At score 4.0, the scale identifies a learning target that clearly exceeds the standard at score 3.0: "The student will solve an engineering problem involving decisions about which material, based on its properties, will best satisfy a set of requirements and constraints." Learning targets at score 4.0 of a high-quality proficiency scale represent application of the target learning. In applying the knowledge or skill from score 3.0 to a new situation beyond what they learned in class or beyond the requirements of the target content, students performing at score 4.0 on the scale engage in new thinking, reasoning, and applying rather than recalling what they were taught. It is important to note that because score 4.0 indicates application of the target content, students may demonstrate proficiency at this level in any number of ways. Specific activities listed at score 4.0 on a proficiency scale are examples only.

The proficiency scale also includes score 1.0 and score 0.0. Score 1.0 on the scale identifies students who need help to demonstrate some of the performance expected at score 2.0 or score 3.0. This has important implications for using the proficiency scale as the basis of assessment design. Because there is no specific score 1.0 content, teachers do not create assessment items that measure student thinking at score 1.0. A student requiring help to correctly answer some or all the 2.0 and 3.0 items would be identified as performing, on that assessment, at score 1.0. Score 0.0 indicates that students cannot demonstrate any knowledge of the learning targets, even with help from the teacher. Finally, some scales (including the example in figure I.1, page 3) use half-point scores between each level, which allow specificity of feedback for students.

It should be clear from this discussion of proficiency scales that the learning targets called out at each level of the scale represent qualitative differences in student cognitive performance rather than quantitative differences. In other words, student performance at each level of the proficiency scale constitutes a different degree of understanding or skill rather than a specific number of correct answers on an assessment.

The proficiency scale is a learning progression, identifying steps students will take in reaching the standard at score 3.0. Thus, teachers can use the scale as the basis of an instructional cycle (which we discuss next, page 6) or unit plan. Following a pretest to determine where students are beginning their learning journey on the scale's learning progression, instruction typically begins at score 2.0. Lessons identify the foundational information and skills and present this information in small chunks, followed by opportunities for students to deepen this basic knowledge (Marzano, 2017). Once students master score 2.0, they are ready for more rigorous lessons on the score 3.0 learning targets. It is with this approach to the design and delivery of an instructional cycle that proficiency scales also identify the content that teachers will assess.

Marzano (2018) spoke directly to the use of proficiency scales informing the process of classroom assessment: "A teacher should be able to transform a well-designed proficiency scale into multiple assessments on a specific topic" (p. 29). In other words, proficiency scales are the structure that supports the development of high-quality classroom assessment. Proficiency scales guide teachers in several critical aspects of assessment development. Because the levels of the scale are organized into progressions of learning that represent different levels of cognitive demand, scales guide teachers in developing assessment items that reflect the cognitive demand indicated in each level. Additionally, assessment items that align with learning targets on a proficiency scale produce an assessment that is standards based, given that a proficiency scale builds a progression of knowledge for a standard or a few related standards.

As the cycle of instruction progresses, teachers will use the scales as a basis for feedback as well. With respect to this practice, students need to reference the proficiency scale itself. Scales can appear in the classroom in a variety of ways, whether projected onto a screen from the teacher's computer, displayed in poster form on a bulletin board, or in the form of printed copies that students can have in front of them. While printed copies are highly effective for student reference, they should normally be supported by some form of large display of the scale in the room. Displaying the scale suggests the importance the teacher sees in the scale, and a display has the additional benefit of making the scale available for reference at every moment of class activity.

Another key way to make proficiency scales available to students is to create student-friendly versions of scales. Because academic standards and the proficiency scales based on them are designed for adults, "the language of learning targets on proficiency scales is typically very appropriate for teachers but may not have a lot of meaning to students" (Hoegh, 2020, p. 50). Teachers can easily translate proficiency scales into more age-appropriate terminology by starting learning targets with "I can" (instead of "The student will"), stripping out extra explanatory elements, and making the format of the scale look more approachable (Hoegh, 2020).

While we strongly recommend the use of proficiency scales as just described, we acknowledge that some schools and districts do not use them. When this is the case, it is paramount that a different process be used to determine learning progressions that form the basis of instruction, assessment, and feedback. This is the essence of standards-based learning. Two other options we will mention here are progressions of knowledge and unpacked standards.

Progressions of knowledge are very similar to proficiency scales, just without numeric values assigned to the levels. The progression begins with a very basic level of performance, progresses to a performance that aligns with the expectations of the standard, and finishes with a complex level of performance. An example appears in figure I.2 (page 6), with the basic level in the bottom section of the chart, the target performance in the middle section, and the advanced level at the top.

Standard: The physically literate individual exhibits responsible personal and social behavior that respects self and others and recognizes the value of physical activity for challenge, self-expression, and social interaction (12.PE.3).

Evaluate self and others regarding attributes of personal and social responsibility.
Demonstrate attributes of personal and social responsibility, including: • Bringing and wearing appropriate physical education (PE) attire   • Putting forth best effort in classroom activities   • Supporting the learning of all students   • Respecting equipment and using it safely   • Listening to and following directions
Describe attributes of personal and social responsibility.

Source for standard: Wyoming Department of Education, 2020.

Figure I.2: Sample progression of knowledge, high school physical education.

Unpacked standards are simply standards that teachers have broken down into their component learning targets. Consider the kindergarten mathematics standard, K.CC.3: "The student will write numbers 0–20 and represent a number of objects with a written numeral 0–20 with 0 (zero) representing a count of no objects" (National Governors Association Center for Best Practices [NGA] & Council of Chief State School Officers [CCSSO], 2010b). A teacher or team might unpack this standard into a number of learning targets, as follows.

- Write numbers from 0 to 20.

- Write the number of objects they see from 0 to 20.

- Copy numbers from 0 to 20.

- Match the number of objects to the correct number.

- State that 0 is a number that shows no objects.

- Tell the meaning of important words, including *object*, *numeral*, *ten frame*, and *zero*.

Once teachers unpack a standard into a collection of learning targets, they can use this information similarly to the learning targets on a proficiency scale. In both cases, each learning target receives significant attention during the instructional process and will be assessed at some point.

Throughout the rest of this book, we describe assessments based on proficiency scales because we believe that scales eliminate a good deal of the work for teachers in understanding the details of the learning progression for each priority standard.

Instructional Cycles

Instruction based on proficiency scales (or other learning progressions) proceeds in what we term *instructional cycles*. An instructional cycle is simply an increment of time when the learning targets on a proficiency scale, or a few related proficiency scales, receive focused instruction. Some educators use the term *instructional unit* rather than *cycle*. Instructional cycles are part of effective instructional planning, which includes three phases. The first phase is yearlong or course-long planning, in which educators identify the priority standards and scales that will receive instructional focus and the approximate amount of time they will spend teaching each scale. The second phase is instructional-cycle planning, when teachers design instructional cycles by identifying the focal proficiency scales for the unit, planning assessments, setting goals for the unit, and so on. The third phase of effective instructional planning is daily lesson planning, meaning that a teacher or team of teachers determines the activities, assignments, and assessments that make up a single class period. For more information about effective instructional planning, see *Planning and Teaching in the Standards-Based Classroom* (Flygare, Hoegh, & Heflebower, 2022).

Teachers instruct in a series of cycles of instruction throughout the semester or year. The sequence of these cycles is often determined by a *curriculum map*, which teachers or teams create after identifying priority standards and proficiency scales for the content area and grade level or the course. The sample curriculum map for high school English language arts (ELA) shown in figure I.3 (page 8) is an example of the first phase of effective instructional planning described previously. This plan identifies the standards that will receive instructional focus during specific instructional cycles over the course of the academic year.

The curriculum map identifies the priority standards taught during a given cycle of instruction and may identify additional supporting standards that teachers should address during instruction. Generally, only the priority standards will have aligned proficiency scales. These scales inform the instruction for the cycle as well as the assessments that teachers will design and administer during the cycle. These assessments will consist of a preassessment, periodic checks for understanding, and an end-of-cycle assessment. We should also note that it is best practice in standards-based teaching to begin instruction with a lesson on the proficiency scale itself (Flygare et al., 2022). In other words, teach the structure and function of the scale and make it a centerpiece of instruction, referring to the levels of the scale as often as possible during instruction, especially when providing students with feedback on their progress. This is essential to using standards-based assessments as a teaching tool. Students' understanding of the scale will change their approach to learning. They are likely to see assessments as opportunities to understand how their learning is progressing rather than a moment to measure their success in the class (Flygare et al., 2022). The design, administration, and scoring of these assessments, along with guidance on how to use data from assessments and give feedback to students, are the topics we address in the chapters that follow.

How to Use This Book

We believe that educators, especially classroom teachers, need to be well versed on what constitutes high-quality assessment practices, including how to select or develop tools and practices that provide data worthy of examination. This is especially important given the fact that all schools and districts have a primary responsibility to lead students to mastery of the standards. In other words, standards-based learning is a non-negotiable

Grand Island Senior High English Language Arts

Yearlong Plan for English 3

Instructional Cycle 0 Setting Goals and Diagnostics	Instructional Cycle 1 Allegory, Characterization, and Theme	Instructional Cycle 2 Rhetoric and Argument
Common texts: • Getting to know you • Expectations, success criteria, and strategies • Measures of Academic Progress (MAP) testing • Diagnostics	Common texts: • *The Crucible* Additional text options: • "Facing Our Fears" • Academy-specific selections by teacher	Common texts: • The Declaration of Independence • The preamble to the U.S. Constitution • The Bill of Rights Additional text options • "Writing Freedom" • Academy-specific selections by teacher
5–7 blocks	**12–15 blocks**	**12–15 blocks**
Standards included in cycle: • RL 11–12.3 Impact of author's choices • RI 11–12.3 Analyzing key details • RI 11–12.5 Analyzing structure • RI 11–12.6 Author's point of view and use of rhetoric • W 11–12.10 Writing routinely • SL 11–12.1 Collaborative discussions • L 11–12.1 Grammar and usage	Standards included in cycle: • RL 11–12.2 Central theme • RL 11–12.3 Impact of author's choices • RL 11–12.6 Point of view • RL 11–12.7 Analyzing interpretations • RL 11–12.9 Author's use of source material • SL 11–12.1 Collaborative discussions • L 11–12.4 Determine meaning of unknown words • L 11–12.5 Figurative language • W 11–12.6 Use technology to produce, publish, and update individual or shared writing products	Standards included in cycle: • RL 11–12.1 Cite evidence • RL 11–12.4 Determine meaning of words • RI 11–12.8 Seminal documents and current events understanding • RI 11–12.9 Seminal documents and current events analysis • W 11–12.2e Informative and explanatory tone • W 11–12.6 Use technology to produce, publish, and update individual or shared writing products • W 11–12.8 Gather relevant information • W 11–12.9 Using information from texts • L 11–12.1 Grammar and usage

Source: © 2021 by Grand Island Public Schools. Used with permission.

Figure I.3: Sample curriculum map, high school ELA.

undertaking for all educators, and assessment is the way educators measure students' progress relative to the standards. Our goal in writing this book is to provide adequate and practical assessment information that fosters teachers' confidence in their ability to create assessments and in the results those assessments produce. To produce a quality and practical resource for teachers and other educators, we draw on the work of many colleagues and experts from the field. In particular, Robert J. Marzano's work on assessment and proficiency scales is prominently represented throughout the book as an influential part of our framework for standards-based classroom assessment.

Chapter 1 lays a foundation of understanding regarding the role of assessment in the standards-based classroom. Chapter 2 details what to assess, when to assess, and how to assess throughout an instructional cycle. In chapter 3, we discuss practices for the design and administration of assessments that improve their quality and consistency, particularly when teachers work in collaborative teams. To delve deeper into assessment quality, chapter 4 reviews characteristics of technically sound assessments and strategies teachers can use to apply these concepts in the classroom. Chapter 5 outlines the process of scoring assessments using a standards-based approach. Chapter 6 acknowledges that assessment is only worthwhile if teachers effectively use the data it generates to respond to students' learning needs, and we provide strategies for doing so. Finally, in chapter 7, we explore giving feedback to students to ensure each assessment opportunity leads to more learning. In its totality, this book contains everything needed to ensure high-quality classroom assessment practices.

1

The Role and Purpose of Classroom Assessment

> Key idea: Assessment plays two ongoing roles during the teaching and learning process—to inform student learning and to monitor the effectiveness of instruction.

Assessment is first and foremost a teaching tool, despite many educators considering it primarily a grading tool. Assessment certainly plays a role in the grading process; however, we must never lose sight of the fact that assessment is one of the most valuable tools in a teacher's toolbox. It is a tool to inform teaching and learning. This is especially important in a standards-based teaching and learning environment. Standards-based learning requires students to make progress toward and ultimately demonstrate mastery of standards, and classroom assessment provides the feedback between students and teachers regarding progress toward that goal (Marzano, 2017). Throughout this book, we approach the use of assessment in this manner, identifying ways in which teachers can use assessments for designing lessons, providing high-quality feedback, evaluating performance and growth, improving instruction, and so on. As such, classroom assessment influences both student behavior and teacher behavior (Marzano, 2010). Specifically, students gain information about "the specific content they must improve on and things they might do to improve" (Marzano, 2010, p. 33). In other words, assessments should tell students and their teachers how individual students are progressing in their learning and where they need to go next.

For teachers, "behavior change involves identifying content that must be reviewed or retaught" (Marzano, 2010, p. 33). They should use assessments to consider whether their instruction is effective and what adjustments they might make to ensure all students learn. Assessment informs the next steps teachers and students take and enhances the learning process. In this chapter, we review these two primary purposes of assessment: (1) to inform student progress and (2) to monitor the effectiveness of instruction.

Informing Student Progress

Even the most traditional conceptions of assessment view it as a way to gain information about students. However, in standards-based environments, assessment informs the entire learning process rather than simply assigning a grade at the end. This occurs through two common uses of assessment (Ferriter, 2020).

1. **Formative assessment:** Assessment that occurs throughout the learning process to inform teaching and learning *while* the learning is taking place.

2. **Summative assessment:** Assessment used at or near the end of an instructional cycle or unit to determine learners' status regarding the topics they were asked to learn during the unit.

Formative and summative assessment are sometimes thought of as different types of assessment. We emphasize that the difference is actually in the use of the assessment results: "In fact, it would be accurate to say that, in general, a specific assessment is neither formative nor summative—it all depends on how the information is used" (Marzano, 2010, p. 27).

Understanding formative and summative uses of assessment also applies to the work of a collaborative team. A *common assessment* is any assessment jointly developed by two or more educators with the intended purpose of collaboratively examining the results to monitor student learning and make necessary adjustments during the learning process. How the team uses those results determines whether the assessment is formative or summative. The approach to assessment we describe also relates directly to one of the key questions that drive the collaborative team process: How will we know students are learning? (DuFour, DuFour, Eaker, Many, & Mattos, 2016). The phrase *are learning* indicates that the purpose of assessment should be to discover whether students are, in fact, progressing throughout instruction. When the concepts of common assessment and formative assessment combine, they empower a team to monitor if students *are learning*.

In the following sections, we discuss formative and summative uses of assessment.

Formative Assessment

Assessment expert Susan M. Brookhart (2016) explained, "Formative assessment is about forming learning—that is, it is assessment that gives information that moves students forward. If no further learning occurred, then whatever the intention, an assessment was not formative" (p. 102). Formative assessment is more commonly used in a standards-based classroom. This category of assessment provides timely data for teachers and learners to examine their understanding of specific aspects of the content, leading toward mastery of the standard. The use of formative assessment in the standards-based classroom allows teachers to adjust instruction and correct misunderstandings that could slow or derail student progress toward the standard. Hanover Research (2014) addressed the concept of formative assessment from the perspective of the learners. They identified three key questions formative assessment must answer for learners:

> **Where am I trying to go?** Students need clearly articulated, concise learning targets to be able to answer this first question. Learning is easier when students understand the goal they are trying to achieve, the purpose of

achieving the goal, and the specific attributes of success. Teachers should continually help students clarify the intended learning as the lessons unfold—not just at the beginning of a unit of study.

Where am I now? All of these strategies help students ascertain—and, even more important, learn how to ascertain—where they are and where they need to be, an awareness that is central to their ultimate success.

How do I close the gap? Assessment for learning helps students know what to do to move from their current position to the final learning goal. To meet learning goals, students must participate fully in creating the goals, analyzing assessment data, and developing a plan of action to achieve the next goal. (Hanover Research, 2014, pp. 4–5)

These three questions indicate that classroom assessment should be an ongoing and continual process that informs not only teachers but also students about their progress or lack of progress in learning. In particular, the term *ongoing* "reinforces that formative assessment is a classroom process that is enacted while the learning is occurring, not something done after the learning has taken place" (CCSSO, 2018, p. 3).

To effectively plan and execute ongoing formative assessment, teachers and learners must have clarity regarding the desired outcome for the learning. Influential proponent of evidence-based education John Hattie (2012) referred to this concept as *targeted learning*, which "involves the teacher knowing where he or she is going with the lesson and ensuring that the students know where they are going. These pathways must be transparent for the student" (p. 52). As described in the introduction (page 1), proficiency scales serve this purpose by defining a learning progression for each topic. Thus, they serve as the basis for assessment as well. Teachers should construct assessments for specific proficiency scales and individual assessment items that relate to specific learning targets. As assessment expert Bill Ferriter (2020) noted, "Tying questions to specific essential learning targets and testing for common misconceptions makes it possible for teachers to use item analyses to quickly identify outcomes that individual students are struggling to master" (p. 93).

When teachers target assessments to proficiency scales, they develop some classroom assessments to specifically measure a single level on a proficiency scale or even an individual learning target within a level. This approach empowers teams to assess learning with shorter, more targeted assessments and to respond to the data from those assessments more immediately. This is especially true when a teacher is trying to cultivate formative assessment data within specific aspects of the learning progression. For example, a teacher might develop an assessment for only the score 2.0 learning targets in a scale to ascertain whether students have grasped the foundational concepts or need more time on these concepts. Likewise, a teacher might use a problem-based assessment task to assess a score 4.0 learning target.

Assessment purpose also usually depends on where the class is in the instructional cycle. Early in the cycle, the teacher may wish to be certain that students' understanding of the simpler content (score 2.0) is solid enough to begin instruction on score 3.0 learning targets. As the instructional cycle proceeds, the purpose of the assessment shifts, with the most recent learning targets and their instruction receiving the focus and previous targets moving into a review capacity. At the end of the instructional cycle, the assessment often becomes more comprehensive and covers multiple levels of the scale. However, it is not a requirement to develop classroom assessments that include items for multiple levels. It is more important for classroom assessments to be appropriately targeted to specific learning outcomes than to include all levels of a scale in a single assessment.

Summative Assessment

Summative assessment serves as a measurement of student knowledge at or near the end of the learning opportunity for a specific topic. In other words, summative assessment results summarize student growth over the course of the instructional unit. The data from a summative assessment should also confirm the student learning that the teacher observed and tracked through formative assessments during the learning process. This accumulation of information that provides a window into student learning throughout an instructional cycle is referred to as *mounting evidence* (Marzano, 2018).

In *A Teacher's Guide to Standards-Based Learning*, authors Tammy Heflebower, Jan K. Hoegh, Philip B. Warrick, and Jeff Flygare (2019) discussed the concept of mounting evidence:

> The thing to remember is that scores may be based on a variety of evidence that indicates a student's learning. These scores may be from obtrusive assessments, or they may include a collection of informal conversations, unobtrusive assessments, or student-generated examples of evidence. It is important to note that relying heavily on a few assessment scores during a grading period may actually increase the error of the evaluative decision— the summative grade. To arrive at a summative grade the teacher uses the concept of mounting evidence by examining the pattern of scores from assessments and assignments for a particular topic or standard. (pp. 86–87)

Teachers can use this mounting evidence to calculate a *summative score* for a specific student by considering all the information across multiple formative assessments; if the mounting evidence clearly shows that a learner has mastered the concepts, the teacher may not need to formally administer a summative assessment. Of course, using a formal summative assessment is always an option, and the results should reflect the growth observed across the series of formative assessments if learners have mastered the content.

Monitoring the Effectiveness of Instruction

Author and expert on learning environments Frederick Erickson (2007) described formative assessment as "the continual taking stock that teachers do by paying firsthand observational attention to students during the ongoing course of instruction—careful attention focused upon specific aspects of a student's developing understanding" (p. 187). This definition implies an important aspect of classroom assessment: teachers' monitoring the effectiveness of teaching strategies as they are using them (Marzano, 2017; Marzano, Rains, & Warrick, 2021). Just as assessment guides student learning, teachers should also use assessment to guide their instruction. In the process of standards-based teaching and learning, it is critical that teachers recognize student understanding and misunderstanding and then adjust instructional activities accordingly. Educators refer to this in general terms as *checking for understanding* or *progress monitoring*. What gets lost in these general descriptions are the cause-and-effect actions teachers should take to generate improved learning: reteaching a specific concept that students misunderstood, speeding up instruction if learners are ready, or providing different examples or modalities for students when the first approach to help them grasp a concept was not successful. Those actions are informed by formative assessment data.

Robert J. Marzano, Cameron Rains, and Philip B. Warrick (2021) offered three categories for monitoring the effectiveness of any instructional activity.

1. **Students' actions:** Behaviors a teacher should expect to see and hear if an instructional strategy is accomplishing what it is supposed to accomplish

2. **Direct questions to students:** Questions a teacher will ask to probe the understanding of the content students are gaining as they engage in a specific learning activity

3. **Artifacts or products:** Tangible evidence of student learning as a result of a specific learning activity

If students produce the expected behaviors, responses to questions, or artifacts following instruction, teachers can determine that the activity or instructional strategy had the desired effect on student learning.

This use of assessment works best with some planning, but it is an efficient process because teachers often use specific teaching activities multiple times within a single school year. Teachers can plan assessment strategies for specific types of instructional activities in advance and then employ them whenever they use those specific activities (Marzano, 2017). Additionally, by planning for the three categories of feedback (students' actions, direct questions to students, and products or artifacts), teachers develop options they can select to use in different situations or to probe the effectiveness of an activity in multiple ways. Figure 1.1 provides an example of how a teacher might plan to assess the effectiveness of activities in which students record or represent new content they are learning.

Student Actions	Direct Questions to Students	Artifacts or Products
• Students actively record content in the correct format, such as notes or graphic organizers. • Students share accurate summaries of information they have recorded.	• What are two of the most important pieces of information you have recorded so far?	• Nonlinguistic representations of the content accurately depict the concepts being taught.

Source: Adapted from Marzano et al., 2021.

Figure 1.1: Sample assessment strategies for monitoring instructional effectiveness as students record and represent new content.

During this lesson, the teacher moves around the room and listens to students discussing the critical information they just explored. Perhaps the teacher hears accurate summaries of the information students have recorded up to this point in time (students' actions). If the teacher wants to know a little more about whether the lesson was effective, he might choose to ask several students the preplanned direct question. By planning the three different methods to assess instructional effectiveness in advance, he has given himself a choice of assessment tools to select from as he monitors learning anytime he uses this type of activity. This form of assessment throughout the learning process provides the opportunity to react immediately if students are not learning.

The CCSSO (2018) also addressed the concept of assessment to monitor instructional effectiveness as a vital piece of the teaching and learning process:

> The emphasis on the planned nature of formative assessment draws attention to the work that teachers should engage in prior to being in the classroom with students. Teachers are able to capitalize on opportunities when observing students engage with a task or during the flow of a discussion that allows a teacher to identify an emerging idea that he or she has not anticipated. (p. 3)

In other words, teachers and teacher teams should use immediate, ongoing assessment to recognize whether the instructional activities they are using are accomplishing the intended effects for learners. When collaborative teams take this approach to assessment, teachers can compare instructional strategies and learn from each other to improve their lessons:

> Assessment data that teams collect also provide practitioners with tangible evidence of the impact their teaching is having on learners. Sometimes data indicate an individual teacher has discovered an instructional strategy that helps more students learn at higher levels. In this case, collaborative team members amplify the strategy, integrating it into the work happening in every classroom to ensure all students have access to the highest-quality learning experiences. (Ferriter, 2020, pp. 113–114)

The process of teachers learning from one another's successes and increasing their instructional competence is an important activity within the collaborative process (Marzano, Heflebower, Hoegh, Warrick, & Grift, 2016). Teams should share effective instructional practices, and the way teachers know which practices are effective is through formative assessment of student learning.

Summary

In this chapter, we reviewed two primary purposes of assessment with a distinct emphasis on the use of formative assessment and its key role in the teaching and learning process. In the standards-based classroom, teachers do not assess students only to assign grades. Rather, assessment is an ongoing process that informs student progress and allows teachers to monitor the effectiveness of their instruction, even to the point of monitoring the effectiveness of specific instructional strategies. With these formative approaches, teachers can adjust throughout a unit to correct misunderstandings, try alternate instructional strategies, intervene when students are falling behind, and provide extension for students who have reached proficiency. Assessment is an integral part of the teaching and learning process. With this understanding, we can turn to the practical details, beginning with how to include assessments throughout the instructional cycle.

Chapter 1 Reflection Questions

1. What are the two primary purposes of assessment? Describe each one.

2. What is the difference between a traditional approach to assessment and assessment in the standards-based classroom?

3. What determines whether an assessment is formative or summative?

4. How can teachers plan to assess the effectiveness of an instructional activity or strategy?

5. Thinking of a unit you have taught or currently teach, how might you apply the concepts or strategies discussed in this chapter?

2

Assessment Throughout the Instructional Cycle

Key idea: Using assessment to inform, enhance, and guide the teaching and learning process enables teachers and teams to discover whether students are learning and make timely adjustments. We will explore when to assess, what to assess, and the different types of assessments teachers can use.

This chapter focuses on the use of classroom assessments in teaching and learning processes throughout the instructional cycle. In standards-based classrooms, it is paramount that teachers monitor learning in an ongoing manner. Therefore, assessment will be a prominent occurrence not just at the end of a unit but during every phase of the instructional cycle. The data from these assessments inform instruction, ensuring that students' needs are met so they can master the priority standards.

The concepts we address focus heavily on formative assessment. To build on the understanding of formative assessment shared in chapter 1 (page 11), consider the following definition.

> Formative assessment is a planned, ongoing process used by all students and teachers during learning and teaching to elicit and use evidence of student learning to improve student understanding of intended disciplinary learning outcomes and support students to become self-directed learners. Effective use of the formative assessment process requires students and teachers to integrate and embed the following practices in a collaborative and respectful classroom environment:
>
> - Clarifying learning goals and success criteria within a broader progression of learning;
>
> - Eliciting and analyzing evidence of student thinking;
>
> - Engaging in self-assessment and peer feedback;
>
> - Providing actionable feedback; and
>
> - Using evidence and feedback to move learning forward by adjusting learning strategies, goals, or next instructional steps. (CCSSO, 2018, pp. 2–3)

This definition supports the idea of ongoing assessment and data use in the standards-based classroom for the sake of optimal student learning.

Within this chapter, we address specific assessment strategies teachers can employ that are in direct alignment with the CCSSO's definition of formative assessment. We also provide ideas and examples of assessment strategies for individual teachers and collaborative teacher teams to consider in their assessment practices.

Assessments Within the Instructional Cycle

Because assessment is an integral part of the standards-based instructional process rather than an activity that takes place in addition to instruction, assessment should occur throughout the instructional cycle. Limiting assessment to the end of the instructional cycle is inadequate. It does not provide enough information about student progress or how well lessons are working. As mentioned in chapter 1 (page 11), teachers must continually collect evidence to make decisions about student learning and eventually to assign an accurate summative score. Collecting mounting evidence requires multiple assessments of learning at different points in the instructional cycle. So what should teachers assess, and when should they assess it?

What to Assess

When considering what to assess, the most obvious answer is, "What you have taught"—in other words, the learning targets on which the teacher has just provided instruction. Fortunately, in the standards-based classroom, priority standards and proficiency scales provide concrete guidance as to what to assess during any given assessment opportunity. In general, teachers will assess any content included in the proficiency scale's learning targets at some point in the instructional cycle. Proficiency scales, because they identify the essential learning for the instructional cycle, identify content that *must* be taught and assessed.

In a standards-based environment, assessments and assessment items are explicitly tied to the content and the levels of the proficiency scale, which are themselves elements of the academic standards. A teacher might decide to give an assessment only covering the score 2.0 content—vocabulary and basic concepts and skills—near the beginning of a unit if those are the only learning targets for which the students have yet received instruction. Assessments on score 3.0 and score 4.0 content come later. While it is often appropriate to concentrate assessment opportunities on specific levels of individual proficiency scales, teachers can also choose to assess all levels on an assessment (score 2.0, score 3.0, and score 4.0), regardless of whether they have taught those targets yet. This gives teachers a complete picture of all students' knowledge and provides additional extension opportunities for students who are learning ahead of pace. When an assessment covers multiple levels of the proficiency scale, the items are typically separated into distinct sections for each level.

When students are used to traditional forms of assessments, placing questions on an assessment that they have little chance of answering correctly can seem unfair. But with standards-based assessments, students will come to understand that the entire purpose and structure of such assessments is different. Traditional assessments often present a series of assessment items based on learned content, and students may be unaware of the cognitive challenge represented by any one assessment item. Each item is usually worth a certain number of points. The object of such an assessment, from the student's point of view, is to get as many points as possible. In this case, assessment items regarding knowledge or skills for which students have not received instruction will likely frustrate them, since they have little chance of answering the item correctly; thus, they will lose the points they might have been able to achieve.

A standards-based assessment presents assessment items that are identified at each level of the proficiency scale. Because students are familiar with the concept of the proficiency scale, they understand that each level represents a different level of cognitive demand or complexity. The object of a standards-based assessment is not to gain as many points as possible. The object of a standards-based assessment is to identify the student's current position on the proficiency scale, representing the acquisition of knowledge and skills as a series of learning targets for a particular standard. In that sense, there is no risk in trying every assessment item. If the student gets the item wrong, they don't lose any points. Scoring assessments in a standards-based method results in teachers knowing more about how students are performing in relation to the standards they're assessing. Teachers then share this information with individual students so they know their current levels of performance and how to improve. (See chapter 5, page 87, for more detail on scoring.) It merely shows what a student has and has not yet mastered on the proficiency scale.

When considering what to assess, teachers might wonder if they should discontinue assessment of learning targets once students have mastered them. Usually, the answer is no. Learning targets that are taught and assessed early in the instructional cycle are typically essential building blocks for later learning, either in the current instructional cycle or later ones. These learning targets will likely play an indirect role in assessments of more complex content. Teachers can also continue assessing earlier learning targets to ensure the knowledge or skill has not degraded. Teachers should consider, however, reducing the frequency of reassessing these learning targets, since the purpose of such assessment is simply to check retention.

Sometimes teachers also choose to include learning targets from earlier units that they have previously assessed to ensure retention of the content. For example, a teacher may have students participate in a bell-ringer activity that addresses content from a previous instructional cycle. Or, the teacher might use an exit slip for the same reason. Some teachers include a review section on formal assessments. The items included in this section pertain to content from earlier instructional cycles. These and other strategies provide information to the teacher and students about degree of retention.

An additional consideration occurs when the curriculum map indicates that a single cycle of instruction should address more than one proficiency scale. This is often the case, particularly at the secondary level, where content areas have different strands of standards that integrate throughout the year. For example, an ELA teacher might instruct a unit on American poetry that includes a reading standard, a writing standard, and a speaking and listening standard, each of which has its own proficiency scale. The teacher would still assess the learning targets covered in class and align individual items to those learning targets, regardless of the scale from which they come. This means that a single assessment might include assessment items that address a reading learning target and a writing learning target.

In some cases, a single assessment task might assess multiple learning targets. This most often occurs with essay prompts and performance assessments. The aforementioned ELA teacher might use an essay assignment to assess a reading standard on interpreting a poem and a writing standard on structuring an interpretive essay. Students' essays would allow the teacher to evaluate their ability to interpret the poem and to create a written piece that presents that interpretation in a logical and well-developed format. In this case, the student would receive two scores, one aligned to the proficiency scale for interpreting a poem and one aligned to the proficiency scale for writing an interpretive essay.

When to Assess

In general, it makes sense to assess student learning shortly after instruction related to that learning. This means that assessments follow clusters of lessons designed to provide instruction on specific learning targets. For example, at the start of a cycle of instruction, the teacher will likely begin with lessons on the score 2.0 content, especially the key academic vocabulary terms. A series of lessons would guide students through understanding the definitions of each term, practicing using the terms, and perhaps deepening their knowledge with an application activity. These activities might take one or two classes, depending on the bell schedule and the amount of instructional time devoted to this content. The teacher would then follow this instruction with an assessment, using the data from that assessment to decide whether students understand the terms to the degree that the class might move on to new content.

To be more specific, teachers can include assessments in their instructional cycle plans at various points. Three important stages are as follows.

1. **Preassessments:** Teachers administer preassessments at the beginning of instructional cycles for the purpose of determining students' level of background knowledge.

2. **Checks for understanding:** Checks for understanding occur frequently over the course of a cycle or unit of instruction. The purpose of these assessments is to determine whether students are learning the information as needed to reach proficiency. If these checks provide insight that students are learning at an adequate pace, instruction moves on as planned. If they suggest otherwise, teachers adjust instructional plans to reteach or reinforce the content.

3. **End-of-cycle assessments:** End-of-cycle assessments usually address the learning targets for a given unit and provide teachers with a comprehensive look at whether students have reached proficiency. While an end-of-cycle assessment may include items related to all learning targets, the primary focus on these assessments is score 3.0. The end-of-cycle assessment occurs

near the conclusion of an instructional cycle but not necessarily on the last day. Indeed, providing the assessment a few days before the end of the cycle allows the teacher to use the data from the assessment to design and offer reteaching, reinforcement, or enrichment activities as needed. Students who have reached proficiency (that is, mastered the score 3.0 content) can work on score 4.0 activities while others continue working toward mastering the target content. When teachers are working in collaborative teams, the end-of-cycle assessment is usually a common assessment: "While some teacher teams might share all their assessments, the end-of-cycle assessment especially is most often created, administered, and analyzed collaboratively in an effort to effectively plan how to support students based on the data" (Flygare et al., 2022, p. 46).

To show how these different stages of assessment might be distributed in an instructional cycle, figure 2.1 (page 24) is an eleven-day instructional-cycle plan based on a grade 8 ELA proficiency scale on theme and central idea. The cycle begins with a preassessment and includes checks for understanding over the course of the learning opportunity. Note that the end-of-cycle assessment occurs on day 7, with some students then organized into groups to participate in a score 4.0 activity. The teacher organizes this activity and is available for guidance over the next several days while these students work independently, but most of the teacher's time will be dedicated to working with students who need remedial instruction to master score 2.0 and score 3.0 learning targets.

The following sections provide additional detail on preassessments, checks for understanding, and end-of-cycle assessments.

Preassessments

In almost every learning opportunity, individuals bring some degree of background knowledge, so it can be helpful to determine what (if any) background knowledge exists before presenting new information to learners. This is the premise for beginning an instructional cycle with a preassessment opportunity. Administering a preassessment can prove beneficial to the instructional planning process. For example, suppose a team of seventh-grade ELA teachers is about to begin an instructional cycle on citing textual evidence. Since students would have been introduced to citing textual evidence in earlier grades, the team opts to give a preassessment to determine whether students are bringing the necessary background knowledge to the seventh-grade classroom. If the results of the preassessment suggest adequate background knowledge exists, teachers may choose to begin addressing learning targets at score 3.0 sooner than originally planned. In contrast, if teachers learn that some background knowledge is lacking, they will provide instruction to ensure students acquire this foundational knowledge. In general terms, if the new learning is based on content addressed in a previous grade level or course, a preassessment opportunity can help the teacher or team determine whether some review of foundational knowledge is necessary.

Day 1	Present and explain the proficiency scale for the priority standard for the unit.
	Administer the preassessment.
	Introduce the topic of theme or central idea through lecture and discussion.
	Provide direct instruction on key vocabulary such as *analysis*, *central idea*, *character*, *development*, *objective*, *plot*, *relationship*, *setting*, *summary*, *supporting detail*, *text*, and *theme*. (Score 2.0)
	Homework: read short excerpts and identify characters, setting, and plot elements (Score 2.0)
Day 2	Briefly review content covered on day 1. (Score 2.0)
	Review and correct homework activity. (Score 2.0)
	Model procedure for summarizing a grade-level-appropriate text using a teacher-provided graphic organizer. (Score 2.0)
	Have students practice summarizing a text using a graphic organizer. (Score 3.0)
	Homework: independent practice using a graphic organizer to summarize a grade-level-appropriate text (Score 2.0)
Day 3	Remind students about learning goals and proficiency scales.
	Review and correct homework activity. (Score 2.0)
	Model procedure for analyzing theme or central idea in a text. (Score 3.0)
	Engage students in practicing identifying theme or central idea using elements such as character development, setting, and plot. (Score 3.0)
	Homework: independent practice summarizing text independently and identifying theme or central idea using character development, setting, and plot elements (Score 3.0)
Day 4	Have students assess their current level of knowledge relative to the proficiency scale. (Assessment)
	Conduct comparison activity on topic and theme. (Score 3.0)
	Homework: review for assessment on theme or central idea (Score 3.0)
Day 5	Remind students about learning goals and proficiency scale.
	Administer check for understanding on theme or central idea. (Assessment)
	Introduce concept of development of theme across a complex text. (Score 3.0)
	Model procedure for analyzing development of theme across a complex text. (Score 3.0)
	Engage students in guided practice on tracing development of theme across a complex grade-level-appropriate text. (Score 3.0)
	Homework: independent practice in analyzing development of theme in a complex text (Score 3.0)
Day 6	Remind students about learning goals and proficiency scale.
	Review homework assignment on analyzing development of theme in a complex text. (Score 3.0)
	Have students self-assess their current level of knowledge relative to the proficiency scale. (Assessment)
	Conduct error analysis involving typical mistakes made when tracing development of theme in a complex text. (Score 3.0)
Day 7	Administer end-of-cycle assessment on analyzing development of theme or central idea in a complex grade-level-appropriate text. (Assessment)
	Organize students into groups for analysis of a challenging text for theme or central idea. (Score 4.0)
Day 8	Student groups receive additional reteaching and reinforcement. (Score 2.0 and 3.0)
	Student groups select text for analysis, tracing the development of theme or central idea through literary elements including character, setting, plot elements, tone, and additional literary devices. (Score 4.0)
	Student groups read and analyze text, comparing their findings and formulating a claim for theme or central idea. (Score 4.0)
Day 9	Student groups receive additional reteaching and reinforcement. (Score 2.0 and 3.0)
	Students continue to read and analyze a complex text for evidence supporting their claim for theme or central idea. (Score 4.0)
Day 10	Individual students plan and write their arguments supporting their claim for theme or central idea in the examined text. Students submit these written arguments for teacher review. (Assessment)
	Student groups meet to synthesize the findings of each group member's findings. (Score 4.0)
	Student groups plan presentations on theme or central idea in their complex texts. (Score 4.0)
Day 11	Student groups present their analysis of texts for theme or central idea. (Score 4.0)
	Conduct a whole-class review with feedback on student group presentations of their claims and defense of their claims regarding theme or central idea development in a complex text. (Assessment)

Source: Adapted from Flygare et al., 2022; Marzano, 2017.

Figure 2.1: Instructional-cycle plan for ELA, grade 8.

On the other hand, there are times when it makes little or no sense to administer a preassessment. Consider a sixth-grade science instructional cycle titled "Human Energy," which includes content about the relationships of kinetic energy to the mass and speed of an object. On examining the standards addressed in this cycle, the teacher or team of teachers may recognize that this is brand-new content for students. In such a case, a preassessment may cause frustration for students and actually be fairly meaningless in terms of attaining information about background knowledge. Ultimately, it is important for a teacher or team to consider whether a preassessment will provide helpful information for planning and delivering initial instruction.

Once teachers decide it is prudent to give a preassessment, they can make choices about the format to use, the amount of time to devote, and the content to include. Many assessment formats can serve as preassessments, such as a traditional quiz, a brief class discussion, a journal entry, an exit ticket, and so on (we discuss assessment formats in more detail later in this chapter, page 33). Educators can also use their discretion regarding how much class time to spend on a preassessment based on their perception of how much information they need to collect to know how to begin initial instruction. Most teachers find that they can collect adequate information in a portion of a class period, even as little as ten to fifteen minutes. Regarding the content of preassessments, teachers might choose to include only foundational knowledge (that is, score 2.0 content) on the preassessment. This approach is appropriate when students have minimal previous exposure to the content of the new instructional cycle. On other occasions, a preassessment may include content at the score 3.0 level to give students an opportunity to demonstrate they are already proficient on the topic or standard at hand. For example, a new cycle of instruction may relate closely to a previous cycle. In this case, it makes sense to include items related to score 3.0 learning targets. It is uncommon to include score 4.0 content on a preassessment since it occurs at the very beginning of the learning opportunity. No matter what format, time, and content a teacher or team decides are most appropriate, preassessment offers insight into the instructional process that will unfold from this point in time.

As an example, figure 2.2 (page 26) presents a proficiency scale for a second-grade mathematics instructional cycle on solving word problems with money, and figure 2.3 (page 27) shows the correlating preassessment. The team of teachers instructing this unit decided to give a preassessment because they know that students learned about coins, their values, and adding currency in first grade. For the format of the preassessment, the teachers generated a traditional quiz because they felt it was an easy yet appropriate method for collecting the necessary information. It will take about five to ten minutes for students to complete. The preassessment only addresses the foundational knowledge on the second-grade proficiency scale because that tells the teachers whether students need a review of the content learned in first grade. If students perform well on this assessment opportunity, instruction can begin at the score 3.0 level. If not, the team can begin by reviewing the score 2.0 learning targets.

Standard: 2.MD.C.8	
Score 4.0	• Solve a multistep word problem involving dollar bills, quarters, dimes, nickels, and pennies.
Score 3.0	• Solve word problems involving dollar bills, quarters, dimes, nickels, and pennies.
Score 2.0	• Recognize or recall specific terminology, such as *all together*, *coin*, *decimal*, *remaining*, and *value*.
	• Use $ and ¢ symbols appropriately.
	• Identify coins and their values.
	• Add or subtract different coins to determine how much money there is all together or remaining.

Source for standard: NGA & CCSSO, 2010a.

Source: Adapted from Marzano, Yanoski, Hoegh, & Simms, 2013.

Figure 2.2: Proficiency scale for word problems with money, grade 2 mathematics.

One final note regarding preassessment is that simply providing the proficiency scale for the instructional cycle to students and having them reflect on the learning targets is a perfectly valid form of preassessment. It introduces the proficiency scale to the students and often enlightens students to the fact that they already know something about the content in this new cycle of instruction. It also involves students in *metacognition*, or thinking about their own knowledge and skill (Marzano & Abbott, 2022). A teacher can facilitate this process by giving students printed copies of the proficiency scale so they can highlight each learning target they learned in a previous grade level or course. Another way to engage students in this particular preassessment opportunity is to organize them into small groups and have them discuss whether they have previously experienced each learning target at score 2.0 and score 3.0. Student-friendly scales or checklists of learning targets make self-reflection very easy.

While not required for every instructional cycle, the results of a preassessment can be a means of gaining valuable insight to guide upcoming instruction.

Checks for Understanding

The goal of using periodic checks for understanding is to ensure that the instructional plan aligns with students' current performance. In this sense, checks for understanding are essential to both purposes of assessment discussed in chapter 1 (page 11): informing student progress and monitoring the effectiveness of instruction. Assessment throughout the unit allows teachers to monitor progress and adjust accordingly, which will improve outcomes for that instructional cycle. If teachers wait until the end of a unit to assess students, it is likely that numerous students will perform poorly on that end-of-cycle assessment, in part because intervention did not occur adequately along the way, and there will be no time left to remedy the situation.

Let's reiterate the definition of *assessment* provided earlier: "Anything a teacher does to gather information about a student's knowledge or skill regarding a specific topic" (Marzano, 2010, p. 22). With this definition in mind, it is easy to plan for periodic checks for understanding throughout a cycle of instruction. For example, a teacher may organize

PREASSESSMENT for *Word Problems With Money*

Word Bank: Use the word bank to write the correct name next to the picture and write its value.

quarter	nickel	cent	dime	penny

1. _____ What is the value? _____

2. _____ What is the value? _____

3. _____ What is the value? _____

4. _____ What is the value? _____

____ / 8 Level 2

Figure 2.3: Preassessment for word problems with money, grade 2 mathematics.   continued ➜

Level 2

Find the value of the money and write it on the line.

5. _____ ¢

6. _____ ¢

7. _____ ¢

8. $____.___

____ / 4 Level 2

Source: © 2018 by South Sioux City Community Schools. Used with permission.

students in a partner or group discussion about a current learning target. Following the discussion, the teacher provides a single note card to each student and projects a prompt on the screen. Students write down their responses to the prompt. The teacher collects the note cards when students are finished crafting their responses and examines each student response to determine whether the collective group has acquired the knowledge within the learning target. Or, the teacher may give a more formal check for understanding, such as a three-item quiz for students to complete. A check for understanding may assess a single learning target, an entire level, or an entire proficiency scale. Bottom line, checks for understanding provide information about whether the students have adequately understood the content taught up to this point in time. The results of any check for understanding, regardless of format or time required, are for determining next instructional steps.

Consider the sample instructional-cycle plan for the seventh-grade social studies topic of "Mesopotamia and the Fertile Crescent" in figure 2.4. The cycle is fifteen days in length and includes one priority standard and two supplemental standards. The team of teachers has planned numerous checks for understanding throughout the unit. For example, on

Priority Standard: WH.7.12.1–6.E1.1

Supplemental Standards: WH.7.12.1–6.E1.2, WH.7.12.1–6.E1.3, RH.4

Day of Cycle	Lesson Plan
Day 1	Activate prior knowledge about Mesopotamia and the Fertile Crescent; locate these areas on a map. Give an overview of the unit. Assign map activity.
Day 2	Teach academic vocabulary. Assign vocabulary practice activity. Provide in-class time to read pages 54–57.
Day 3	Check for understanding 1: Check vocabulary knowledge. Provide direct instruction regarding why the development of agriculture led to the creation of cities.
Day 4	Group activity: Creating a farming community. Check for understanding 2: Write a response to the question, "List three ways the development of agriculture led to the creation of cities."
Day 5	Teach academic vocabulary. Assign vocabulary practice activity. Provide in-class time to read pages 60–64.
Day 6	Provide instruction regarding religion and social construct of Sumerian society. Check for understanding 3: Think-pair-share, "How did trade affect Sumerian society? How does it still affect society today?"
Day 7	Provide in-class time to read section 3. Partner activity: Generate a list of achievements made by the Sumerians. Do we still use any of these today?
Day 8	In-class activity: Write your name in cuneiform (paper and clay). Exit ticket: List three Sumerian achievements, then write a brief paragraph (three to five sentences) arguing which you believe to be the most useful and why.
Day 9	Teach academic vocabulary. Provide in-class time to read section 4. Provide direct instruction regarding this section.
Day 10	Teach Hammurabi's Code song (YouTube). Introduce Hammurabi's Code scavenger hunt. Check for understanding 4: Why are written laws important?
Day 11	In-class review of Mesopotamia and the Fertile Crescent
Day 12	End-of-cycle assessment
Day 13	Reteaching, reinforcement, and enrichment
Day 14	Reteaching, reinforcement, and enrichment
Day 15	Reteaching, reinforcement, and enrichment

Source: © 2021 by North Dakota Northeast Education Services Cooperative. Adapted with permission.

Figure 2.4: Instructional cycle for Mesopotamia and the Fertile Crescent, grade 7 social studies.

day 3, students will engage in a check for understanding, which gives the teachers information about student understanding of important academic vocabulary.

Using the information gleaned from each check for understanding, teachers determine the best course of instruction for students. If all students perform well on the assessment, it is prudent to move all students forward in the learning. However, if some students do not demonstrate strong performance, it is important to structure upcoming lessons based on individual student needs. This may mean that the next lesson begins with differentiation time where the students who need additional opportunities to learn receive focused instruction while the students who are ready to move forward work on something different. Once the reteaching opportunity is done, groups can come back together and move forward in the learning. Hence, it is very important that teachers review the data from each check for understanding carefully to plan instruction that supports all learners as best as possible.

End-of-Cycle Assessments

End-of-cycle assessments occur toward the end of an instructional cycle and are more comprehensive and summative in nature, meaning they include items or tasks covering most or all of the content taught in the cycle. For the sake of ensuring alignment to the standard or standards included in the cycle, it is paramount that the proficiency scale or other learning progression serves as the basis for this important assessment opportunity, especially because the end-of-cycle assessment is often a common assessment among a team of educators. The following steps are helpful for generating a high-quality end-of-cycle assessment.

1. Examine the proficiency scale, progression of knowledge, or unpacked standards to stay focused on the required knowledge and skills.

2. Determine the number and type of assessment items required for each learning target. Figure 2.5 shows an example.

3. Locate existing items or create new items to meet the requirements of step 2.

Score 2.0	Score 3.0	Score 4.0
One vocabulary matching set Three multiple-choice items One short-answer item	Two extended constructed-response items	One extended constructed-response item

Figure 2.5: Results of assessment planning, step 2.

Teachers developing assessments commonly ask how to determine the number of assessment items for each level on the proficiency scale. The answer is that it depends on how many items those teachers need to confidently determine whether students have learned the content. While this response does not state an explicit number, it does offer an opportunity for teachers to use their professional judgment regarding what is best for students and what will be adequate information to make a decision about students' current level of performance. When choosing the number of items for each scale level on an end-of-cycle assessment, the following considerations are helpful.

- **The number of checks for understanding prior to the end-of-cycle assessment:** If the teacher has administered numerous checks previously, the end-of-cycle assessment can probably include fewer items related to foundational knowledge already assessed.

- **The assessment item types included on the end-of-cycle assessment:** With selected-response items, more items are needed to ensure that students truly know the content and did not just guess correctly. With constructed-response items, fewer items are typically needed, as students generate responses and possibly draw on their knowledge of multiple learning targets within a single question.

- **The verbs in the standards or learning targets being assessed:** Items should honor the complexity level suggested by the learning targets or standards. For example, if a standard (or score 3.0 learning target) uses the verb *analyze*, then a constructed-response item might be the best match to assess it.

- **The balance of the assessment:** At the end of an instructional cycle, teachers should focus most of the assessment on the level of proficiency—that is, the score 3.0 level of the proficiency scale or the performance required by the standard. After all, that is the content that students must master. The number of foundational (score 2.0) and knowledge application (score 4.0) items should allow students to demonstrate basic knowledge and go beyond proficiency but not be the primary emphasis. While there might be a higher number of foundational items (as they are often short, discrete, selected-response items), the distribution of items should focus students' time and effort toward the target content.

- **The format of the assessment:** End-of-cycle assessments can be traditional written tests, but they do not have to be. Performance tasks are frequently appropriate, and teachers sometimes choose to use informal assessments. We discuss both of these topics in the next section. Teachers should choose methods that give them information about what students know or are able to do based on the requirements of the standards.

As mentioned previously, the end-of-cycle assessment usually occurs near the end of the cycle but not necessarily on the last day of the cycle. This is so the teacher or team can use the data from the assessment to design reteaching, reinforcement, and enrichment activities. For example, if an instructional cycle is sixteen days long, the teacher might give the final assessment on day 13. Because end-of-cycle assessments are often common assessments and heavily weighted in determining summative scores, teams need time to rigorously analyze the assessment results (see Data Protocols, chapter 3, page 63) and plan in response.

As an example of an end-of-cycle assessment, figure 2.6 (page 32) shows a first-grade ELA assessment for elements of literary text. Notice the tight alignment between the learning targets on the proficiency scale and the items on the assessment. Additionally,

Score Level	Learning Target
Score 4.0	Explain how a story would change if a character, the setting, or an event was different.
Score 3.0	Describe the main characters in a story using key details. Describe the setting of a story using key details. Describe the major events in a story using key details.
Score 2.0	Identify the story elements (for example, characters, setting, events). Identify key details within the story. Identify major events in the story.

Please listen to or read the text "A Fishy Adventure." Your teacher will help you write answers to the following questions.

Complete the chart below with words or pictures. (Score 2.0)

1. Who is the main character in the story?	2. What is the setting of the story?

3. What kind of fish is the main character? (Score 2.0)

    a. angelfish   c. dogfish

    b. clownfish   d. lionfish

4. Why is the fish sad at the beginning of the story? (Score 3.0)

5. What key detail from the text helps you know the answer to the previous question? (Score 3.0)

6. Would the main character have the same problem if he was a different type of fish? Why or why not? (Score 4.0)

Source for proficiency scale: © 2016 by Marzano Resources. Adapted with permission.

Figure 2.6: End-of-cycle assessment, grade 1 ELA.

this assessment is rather concise because the learning targets on the proficiency scale are unidimensional (that is, each one encompasses a single idea). For that reason, it is not necessary to include multiple items for each learning target on the assessment—especially since the teacher has previously administered other checks for understanding. Students will likely be assessed on elements of literary text again because of the spiraling nature of ELA—it is a concept that is addressed numerous times over the course of an academic year with different pieces of literary text.

It is important to mention again that assessment can be anything a teacher does to gather information about what a student knows or is able to do (Marzano, 2010). When talking about what (everything) and when (frequently) to assess, it is easy to feel overwhelmed by the perceived amount of time spent in the assessment process. This reminder that assessments do not always need to take significant time can help minimize that feeling.

Assessment Types and Formats

Understanding classroom assessment as part of the teaching and learning process enhances the flexibility with which individual teachers and collaborative teams can use assessment. Our broad conception of what constitutes an assessment adds versatility to the assessment types and formats teachers can employ at all grade levels and in all content areas. Educators are not limited to traditional written exams (though those still have their place). When standards, not grades, are the focus, there are many methods to glean important information about whether students are learning. First, we consider three types of classroom assessment, shown in table 2.1, along with descriptions and examples. Teachers can use any of the three types of assessment in a formative or summative manner. This fact provides teachers with a variety of assessment options for different content or skills, different age groups, and even different individual learners' needs.

Table 2.1: Three Types of Assessment

Assessment Type	Explanation	Examples
Obtrusive Assessment	• Formal in nature • Interrupts the normal flow of activity in a classroom • Students are fully aware this is an assessment event	• Tests and quizzes • Exit tickets • In-class assignments • Oral assessments of individual students
Unobtrusive Assessment	• Informal in nature • Does not stop the flow of learning activities • Students may not realize they are being assessed	• Observations of student performance • Listening for understanding of concepts during student interactions and discussions • Auditing academic journals or portfolios
Student-Generated Assessment	• Students generate or select ideas for demonstrating their knowledge or skills for a specific topic	• Conference with a teacher • Development or demonstration of a student-determined product or performance • Options provided for students on a choice board

Source: Adapted from Heflebower et al., 2019; Marzano, 2010; Marzano & Abbott, 2022.

Within these broad assessment types, classroom assessments typically consist of numerous items and tasks. Every one of these is an important part of the overall assessment; therefore, each needs to be a high-quality item or task. Gareis and Grant (2015) stated:

> Any teacher who has ever written items for a test, a quiz, or a quick check for formatively assessing student learning at the beginning or end of a lesson will attest to the fact that writing a good question that addresses the content and level of cognitive demand of an intended learning outcome can be difficult and time consuming. (p. 91)

In response to this challenge, this section presents some guidance for writing high-quality assessment items and tasks, along with examples of the various types. Visit **www.Marzano Resources.com/reproducibles** for a reproducible overview of this information.

Selected-Response Items

Selected-response items require students to choose the correct answer from listed options. They are popular, familiar, and easy to score. Because they test individual facts or elements of content and do not require students to apply that content, teachers need to use multiple items of this type to know whether a student has really learned the content. Selected-response items are usually most appropriate for assessing score 2.0 content like vocabulary terms and foundational information.

Selected-response items include true or false, matching, multiple choice, and fill in the blank.

True or False

With true-or-false items, students simply determine whether each statement is accurate or inaccurate. To write high-quality true-or-false items, teachers should:

- Relate statements to a single idea

- Ensure items are absolutely true or absolutely false

- Avoid using qualifiers, opinions, and negatives

However, we recommend using this item type sparingly, as students have a fifty-fifty chance of guessing the correct answer. Consider the following examples.

_____ Johann Sebastian Bach was a musician of the late Baroque period.

_____ Two vertical angles form a linear pair.

_____ The Mississippi River is the longest river in the world.

These items are all absolutely true-or-false statements. Additionally, there are no opinions or qualifiers in any of these items.

Matching

Matching items require students to identify which of a set of options best relates to each prompt. When writing matching items, teachers should:

- Keep content homogeneous

- Keep the matching set short

- Include an uneven number of items for students to match or allow items for use more than once

- Format the item with the prompts on the left and the matching options on the right

The following is an example of a high-quality matching item.

Write the letter of each type of figurative language next to the sentence that matches it. One letter will be used twice.

____ Boom! The thunder echoed through the sky.	A. Simile
____ The warm sun peeked out from behind the gray clouds.	B. Metaphor
____ Bees busily buzzed through the blossoms.	C. Hyperbole
____ He was like a gazelle running smoothly down the road.	D. Alliteration
____ The cookies were so delicious that I think I ate a million of them!	E. Onomatopoeia
____ The teacher was a wise owl.	F. Personification
____ The sky opened and cried its tears upon the earth.	

The matching options are all types of figurative language, therefore keeping the content homogeneous. The number of prompts and options is relatively short, and there is a mismatch between the number of options and the number of blanks. Even though this is a simple item type that students are likely familiar with, it is always in students' best interest to provide directions about how to complete the item set. Finally, the item is formatted so that students will only need to read each prompt once, assuming they know the content.

Multiple Choice

Multiple-choice items present students with a prompt and several possible answers, from which students must select the one correct option. Teachers writing multiple-choice questions should:

- Ensure the problem is clear in the item stem
- State the stem in the positive whenever possible
- Emphasize any qualifiers in the stem
- Ensure all answer choices are plausible
- Make answer choices parallel in grammar and length
- Avoid *all of the above* and *none of the above*
- Avoid clues in answer choices
- Ensure only one correct response is possible

The following examples demonstrate these tips.

1. Read the following sentence from the story.

   Around three o'clock, they agreed it was time to pack up the game, so they all <u>pitched in</u> to roll up the mat and push and pull it back to where it was stored.

   Based on the context, what does the underlined phrase mean? Circle the correct response.

   a. forgot   c. played

   b. helped   d. pretended

2. Circle the letters of the three paragraphs that are most relevant to providing an objective summary of the passage.

   a. paragraph 1   e. paragraph 28

   b. paragraph 5   f. paragraph 34

   c. paragraph 9   g. paragraph 45

   d. paragraph 17

3. Circle the letter of the *best* response to the question. For centuries, a young man who wanted to learn a craft was apprenticed to a master craftsman who taught him the necessary skills. Why did the apprenticeship system begin to decline in the first half of the 1800s?

   a. Craftsmen began to use unskilled immigrant labor in their shops.

   b. Many young men chose to become farmers instead of craftsmen.

   c. The growth of the factory system led to a decreased need for skilled labor.

   d. The apprenticeship system was considered unsuitable for the increased number of women working outside the home.

Source for item 3: U.S. Department of Education, 2010.

These items include adequate information for the student, including directions for completing the item. Most prominent in the first two items is the fact that the options are all single words, and they are ordered logically (in alphabetical or numerical order), helping to ensure that no single answer stands out as the obvious correct response. In the third example, the responses are presented in order from shortest to longest response for the same reason. Also, notice that the word *best* is italicized in the directions for item 3 to ensure that students understand there are multiple options that may seem to be the right response, but one response stands out from the others as the best.

Fill in the Blank

Students answer fill-in-the-blank questions by writing the missing word in the space provided. Some fill-in-the-blank items include word banks for students to choose answers from. Even if students must generate the answer, fill-in-the-blank items "are more like selected-response items than short constructed-response items because the answer is so short and focused" (Marzano, 2018, p. 41). When writing fill-in-the-blank items, teachers should:

- Position the blank toward the middle or the end of the sentence
- Limit the number of blanks in a single item to three or fewer
- Ensure blanks are the same length
- Be sure information surrounding the blank provides adequate context

Consider the following examples.

1. The thread-like molecules that carry hereditary information are _____.
2. The three branches of government are _____, _____, and _____.

Notice that the position of the blanks is at the end of the sentence, providing adequate context for the learner. Additionally, in the item with multiple blanks, each blank is the exact same length.

Constructed-Response Items

Another common category of assessment items is constructed response, which requires students to generate a written or verbal response. Constructed-response items minimize the possibility for students to guess the correct response, as choices are not provided. This type of item is typically considered more rigorous as a result. Many learning targets on proficiency scales include verbs that require this type of item, such as *explain*, *describe*, *analyze*, *predict*, *justify*, and many more.

Constructed-response items include short constructed response and extended constructed response.

Short Constructed Response

Also known as *short answer*, short constructed-response items require students to write a single word, a short phrase, or a sentence or two. Additionally, short constructed-response items may require drawings or symbols, especially in primary classrooms. Teachers can tailor short constructed-response items to assess content at any level of the proficiency scale. Teachers writing short constructed-response items should:

- Make the nature of the desired response clear to the student

- Develop scoring criteria for the question

- Provide adequate space for responses

Consider the following example.

> Why does asexual reproduction produce offspring with identical genetic information? Write your answer in the box. You can use a drawing to help explain your answer.

This item would be accompanied by a designated space in which students may craft their answers (in this case, including a drawing if they choose). It is important to note that a short-answer item requires scoring guidance to ensure consistency of scoring (see chapter 3, page 51). For an item such as this example, the most appropriate scoring guidance would be *anchors*, or student responses used as exemplars that teachers refer to during the scoring process. Teachers might select actual student work as anchors or generate the exemplar responses themselves.

Extended Constructed Response

Extended constructed-response items, often taking the form of essay questions, require students to write longer compositions in response to multipart prompts. Therefore, they are most appropriate for score 3.0 and score 4.0 content. When writing prompts for extended constructed responses, teachers should:

- Make the nature of the desired response clear to the reader

- Develop scoring criteria for the question

- Provide adequate space for responses

The following example demonstrates a high-quality extended constructed-response item.

> Based on the information we have learned and any resources of your choosing, write a response to this question:
>
> **Why might historians consider ancient Greece the first Western civilization?**

Use the Claim, Evidence, Reasons format for your response. Also, use the following checklist to ensure you include everything necessary in your response.

- Begin with a claim or thesis statement.

- Include three or more pieces of evidence and supporting reasons.

- End with a concluding statement.

- Include relevant vocabulary (see ancient Greece proficiency scale).

- Include complete sentences and correct capitalization and punctuation.

Source: © 2020 by Christina Nilson and Melinda Struebing. Used with permission.

This extended constructed-response item has multiple parts, so the use of a checklist is helpful to students for ensuring they address everything required in the item. Students might write their responses with pen and paper or using a computer. If it is a pen-and-paper opportunity, the assessment document should provide adequate space or direct students to craft their response on a separate sheet of paper.

Essay assignments are also a form of extended constructed response. Because essay assignments have more complex requirements, it is often appropriate for the teacher to provide a detailed rubric to guide both students' writing and teachers' scoring. Consider the following essay prompt, which corresponds to the proficiency scale in figure 2.7 (page 40). The rubric in figure 2.8 (page 41) details the requirements for the final written product. It is important to note that the integration of content and writing skills inherent in essays makes them similar in some ways to performance assessments (see page 43), which also require rubrics to define clear criteria for the task.

After completing research on the influence of social media on the lives of students, you will write an explanatory article for your school's newspaper. The audience for your article will be fellow students, teachers, administrators, and parents.

Draw your research from multiple sources and develop a thesis for your article on the influence of social media on the lives of students your age. Using multiple sources and accurately citing those sources, present the most relevant information to support your thesis. Write the article in an engaging and well-organized manner, always following your thesis. The article should present the ideas of your sources but should be in your own words unless you are directly quoting your sources. Use proper citations when referencing your sources.

continued ➡

Your explanatory article will be scored using the following criteria.

1. **Thesis:** Establish and state your thesis. Present information logically to develop your thesis throughout the article.

2. **Organization:** Present ideas in a way that develops your thesis and leads to a logical conclusion. Transition smoothly from one idea to the next. Include an effective introduction and conclusion.

3. **Evidence, elaboration, and formatting:** Include relevant information, formatting, and graphics to support your thesis and argument. Present effective evidence to further your argument.

4. **Conventions:** Follow the requirements of grammar usage, punctuation, capitalization, and spelling.

Standards		
W.9–10.2: Write informative and explanatory texts to examine and convey complex ideas, concepts, and information clearly and accurately through the effective selection, organization, and analysis of content.		
W.9–10.2b: Introduce a topic; organize complex ideas, concepts, and information to make important connections and distinctions; include formatting (such as headings), graphics (such as figures or tables), and multimedia to aid in comprehension, if needed.		
Proficiency Scale		
Score 4.0	In addition to score 3.0 performance, the student demonstrates in-depth inferences and applications that go beyond the target content.	
	Score 3.5	In addition to score 3.0 performance, partial success at score 4.0 content
Score 3.0	The student will write informative and explanatory texts to examine and convey complex ideas, concepts, and information clearly and accurately through the effective selection, organization, and analysis of content. The student will introduce a topic; organize complex ideas, concepts, and information to make important connections and distinctions; and include formatting (such as headings), graphics (such as figures and tables), and multimedia to aid in comprehension, if needed.	
	Score 2.5	No major errors or omissions regarding score 2.0 content, and partial success at score 3.0 content.
Score 2.0	The student will recognize or recall specific vocabulary such as *cause and effect, comparison and contrast, format, graphic features, multimedia features*. The student will perform basic processes, such as: • Identify multiple ways to introduce complex ideas • Generate an outline of a well-organized informative and explanatory text • Identify multiple methods of properly formatting an informative and explanatory text • Write informative and explanatory texts following a teacher-provided organizer	
	Score 1.5	Partial success at score 2.0 content, and major errors or omissions regarding score 3.0 content
Score 1.0	With help, partial success at score 2.0 content and score 3.0 content	
	Score 0.5	With help, partial success at score 2.0 content but not at score 3.0 content

Source for standards: Ohio Department of Education, 2017.

Figure 2.7: Proficiency scale for informative and explanatory writing, grades 9–10 ELA.

Score	Thesis and Focus	Organization	Presentation of Evidence and Format	Conventions
4	• Thesis is clearly stated and complete. • Focus is maintained throughout the entirety of the text.	• Organization is clear and effective and directly supports the argument of the text. • Text and its argument are complete. • Transitions are evident and consistently appropriate. • Introduction and conclusion are complete and contribute to the efficacy of the text.	• Thesis is thoroughly supported with relevant evidence. • Ideas are consistently elaborated. • Format consistently supports the argument of the text. • Graphics consistently support the argument of the text.	• Command of conventions is consistently strong. • There are few or no errors in capitalization, punctuation, and spelling.
3	• Thesis is clearly stated. • Focus is maintained through most of the text.	• Organizational structure is evident. • Argument of the text has a sense of completeness. • Work has adequate transitions. • Work has adequate introduction and conclusion.	• The thesis has adequate support. • Ideas are occasionally elaborated. • Format generally supports the argument of the text. • Graphics usually support the thesis.	• There is evidence of general understanding and command of conventions with occasional errors. • Use of capitalization, punctuation, and spelling is adequate.
2	• Thesis is stated, but somewhat unclear. • Focus is only occasionally maintained.	• Organizational structure is not consistently maintained. • Argument may be incomplete. • Transitions are attempted but not consistent.	• Support for thesis is occasional rather than consistent. • Elaboration of ideas is inadequate. • Some format choices support the argument of the text.	• There is evidence of partial understanding of conventions of writing. • There are frequent errors of capitalization, punctuation, and spelling.
1	• Thesis is absent or entirely unclear. • Focus is rarely achieved throughout the piece.	• There is little evidence of organizational structure. • Argument is incomplete. • There is little evidence of transitions from idea to idea.	• There is little or no support for the ideas discussed. • There is little or no elaboration of ideas. • There are few or no formatting choices to support ideas in the text.	• Use of conventions indicates lack of command. • There are frequent and severe errors in capitalization, punctuation, and spelling.
0	The work indicates little or no ability to create an informative and explanatory text.			

Figure 2.8: Analytic rubric for essay assignment.

Discussions With Students

Discussions with students are a very plausible way to assess learning. In essence, the teacher has a conversation with a student to determine what that student knows or is able to do. This assessment type is sometimes misconstrued as impractical because of the amount of time it may take, but even short verbal interactions with students can serve to assess their degree of learning at any level of the proficiency scale.

Personal Communication

Personal communication assessments involve the teacher providing a spoken version of any of the previously described item types. This assessment format is especially prominent in primary classrooms (preK–grade 2) where very young learners are still learning to read. The teacher might simply read the assessment to individual students and have those students answer as if they were completing it independently. Or, the teacher might engage in a conversation with a student or small group of students. In either case, teachers typically design and use a recording sheet of some sort to document the results of the assessment or conversation. The sample recording sheet in figure 2.9 displays student names on the left and the assessment questions across the top. The teacher can easily capture important information collected through the conversation with each learner.

Questioning Sequences

One way to structure discussions with students and integrate assessment into instruction is the idea of a *questioning sequence*, which uses "specific types of questions in an intentional sequence to guide students through the thinking necessary to generate deep understanding of the content and its implications" (Marzano & Simms, 2014, p. 12). Learning occurs through the scaffolding of knowledge and skills. Proficiency scales provide a logical scaffolding of information that teachers can develop into a sequence of questions at different levels of cognitive demand. Robert J. Marzano and Julia A. Simms (2014) identified four phases of questions in their sequencing model, which teachers can use for oral or written interactions with students:

1. Questions about details
2. Questions about categories
3. Questions that require students to elaborate on their previous answers
4. Questions that require students to provide evidence for their elaborations (p. 13)

It is more important that the questions within a sequence be meaningful than numerous. Questions at lower levels in the sequence should connect directly to the knowledge and skills needed for questions at the next level in the sequence. Since proficiency scales provide tiered content within each topic, teachers can develop questioning sequences based on the scales. In so doing, the phases of questioning correlate directly to specific levels on the scale or certain learning targets within a level on the scale. For example, consider the proficiency scale in figure 2.10 (page 44) for telling time to the nearest five minutes. Sample questions, following the questioning sequence previously described, appear in the right-hand column. You will see an obvious increase in the cognitive demand as you read the questions from score 2.0 to score 4.0.

	Key Ideas and Details					
	Story Elements Recording Sheet					
	Y = Yes, student answered correctly		P = Partially correct		N = No, student answered incorrectly	
Student Name	**Score 2.0** What is the setting of the story?	**Score 2.0** Who is (are) the main character(s)?	**Score 3.0** What happened at the beginning, middle, and end of the story?	**Score 4.0** What might have happened if . . .	**Student's Proficiency Level**	**Notes**
Adam E.	Y	P	P	N	1.5	Adam provided one character and only knew what happened at the end of the story.
Leni W.	Y	Y	Y	Y	4.0	Assessment was easy for Leni.
Paulo R.	Y	Y	Y	N	3.0	Paulo was unable to respond to the score 4.0 item.
Suri O.	N	N	P	N	1.5	Suri was able to tell the ending of the story.

Figure 2.9: Sample recording sheet for personal communication assessment.

Remember, instruction based on the proficiency scale prepares students with the knowledge and skills they will be assessed on at the different levels of the scale. A teacher would initiate each level of the questioning sequence as the teacher deems students are ready, which could be as a whole class or individually. Likewise, levels of the questioning sequence can be reused at any time with the entire class, small groups of students, or individual students to assess growth and retention of prior knowledge.

Performance Assessments

Among the most powerful forms of classroom assessment is the performance assessment. This category of assessment includes a wide range of possibilities, but all performance assessments share the characteristic of requiring the student to create a product, either in the form of a physical object or a performance of some kind. Performance assessments often require students to apply their understanding in new situations, different from what

Score 4.0	The student will: • Solve real-world problems involving elapsed time.	Evidence question: *How long was your trip if you leave your house at 9:07 and arrive at your destination at 9:45? How do you know this is the correct answer?*
Score 3.0	The student will: • Tell and write time from analog clocks to the nearest five minutes.	Elaboration question: *Why is it important for people to be able to tell time on an analog clock?*
Score 2.0	The student will: • Recall important terminology, such as: *analog, clock, digital, minute, nearest, time, a.m.,* and *p.m.* • Tell and write time from digital clocks to the nearest five minutes. • Identify the hands on an analog clock. • Count by fives to sixty. • Tell time to the hour, half-hour, and quarter-hour. • Write time using the correct format.	Category question: *How is an analog clock different from a digital clock?* Detail question: *What is an analog clock?*

Source: Adapted from Hoegh, 2020; Marzano & Simms, 2014.

Figure 2.10: Questioning sequence based on a proficiency scale.

they have previously encountered in the classroom. Thus, performance assessment often applies to the upper-level learning targets on the proficiency scale (score 3.0 and score 4.0). Examples of this type of assessment include a science lab, a musical performance, the performance of a skill associated with a particular sport, the creation of an art project, and many others. What makes performance assessment so effective in terms of assessing student achievement is that they often emulate real-life situations (Marzano, 2018).

While some subject areas make more use of performance assessments than others, almost all classrooms have the potential for engaging students in performance tasks. For example, an art student may create a charcoal drawing. In a physical education classroom, students might play soccer for the sake of demonstrating skills such as passing and dribbling the ball. In social studies and science, students commonly present personal research projects. In ELA, essay assignments (as mentioned previously, page 38) are a type of performance assessment.

There are many similarities in the design process between performance assessments and traditional forms of assessment. The proficiency scale is the starting point, and the first question a teacher considers is which learning targets are the focus of the assessment. By choosing the learning targets and aligning the performance assessment to those learning targets, the assessment can provide teachers with specific feedback on students' abilities at a certain point in the learning cycle. Performance assessments include two components: (1) the task itself and (2) the scoring criteria. The scoring criteria, often a rubric or checklist, establishes the requirements of the task in a transparent manner for students.

Because the scoring guidelines are an essential part of a performance assessment, we should examine the similarities and differences between a proficiency scale and a rubric.

At first glance, proficiency scales and rubrics may appear to be alike; they certainly share a great many characteristics. Both identify levels of student performance on a body of content knowledge or skill. Both are designed to specify whether a student is proficient regarding those levels of performance. But unlike a proficiency scale, a rubric is designed for use with a specific assignment or performance assessment (Marzano, 2018). Unlike a rubric, a proficiency scale aligns to a specific priority standard *and* defines levels of student proficiency for multiple types of assignments and assessments across the entire learning progression in which the student will engage. In a standards-based classroom, *both a proficiency scale and a rubric* are usually required for a high-quality aligned performance assessment. The proficiency scale ensures the validity of the performance assessment based on that scale (for more information on assessment validity, see chapter 4, page 67). The rubric ensures students have clarity about the evaluation criteria for the specific task they are doing and provides the opportunity for specific feedback to the students about their own performance on the task.

We recommend the following sequence for designing a performance assessment.

1. Identify the proficiency scale you will assess.

2. Identify the specific learning targets from the scale that you will assess.

3. Create the activity that will constitute the assessment itself. Write the prompt keeping the specific learning targets you will assess in mind.

4. Write the scoring criteria for the performance assessment.

5. Review the rubric and assessment to assure that both align with the scale.

A performance assessment that is properly aligned to a standard can be as simple or as complex as a teacher needs it to be. For example, consider the following sixth-grade ELA writing standard, W.6.2: "Write informative or explanatory texts to examine a topic and convey ideas, concepts, and information through the selection, organization, and analysis of relevant content" (NGA & CCSSO, 2010a). Such a standard is one that a classroom teacher would address different aspects of in various instructional cycles throughout the entire school year. Figure 2.11 (page 47) presents a proficiency scale for this standard.

During an instructional cycle that addresses a portion of this scale, the teacher might use the following essay assignment.

Many people enjoy spending time on a hobby or a sport. Here's your chance to tell the world about an activity you really enjoy!

You will write a short paper describing a sport or hobby you engage in and telling why you like doing it. The paper should be two to four pages in length, and it must include a complete description of the activity with examples from your own experience. Also, you should include a detailed description of how you got started doing the activity, why it appeals to you, and how you have grown in performing the activity over time.

continued →

Here are some specific requirements for the paper:

- ☐ Identify and describe the hobby, sport, or activity.
- ☐ Include specific details of how one performs the hobby, sport, or activity. Tell your audience exactly what you do when you engage in this activity.
- ☐ Describe why you like it, providing specific details.
- ☐ Be sure to include how you got started with it.
- ☐ Tell the reader how you have grown in your performance of this activity.
- ☐ As we have been working on in class, make sure your paper properly introduces the topic and provides relevant supporting details.
- ☐ Match the style of the writing to your audience.
- ☐ Include appropriate transitions within your paper to guide your reader from topic to topic.
- ☐ Make sure you edit for spelling, grammar, and mechanics.

The teacher can also use the checklist included in the prompt as a rubric when analyzing students' essays and giving feedback, perhaps scoring how well students met each criterion on a 1–4 scale. This assessment prompt and its associated checklist are relatively easy to construct and make it easy to provide specific feedback to students on the requirements of the assignment. The assessment is aligned to the standard and assesses that portion of the proficiency scale on which students received instruction in the current instructional cycle.

Teachers may have the misconception that performance assessments are too complex for primary students. When properly executed, performance assessments can be used in primary grades. Consider the following example of a mathematics performance assessment for kindergarten.

The kindergarten teachers have hired you as a children's book author to create a number book for the kindergartners next year, similar to *Ten Little Ladybugs* by Melanie Gerth (2000). You will create a page in your book for each number from zero to ten showing either an addition or subtraction word problem with drawings.

Source: Colorado Department of Education, n.d.c.

This performance assessment is completely age appropriate and will be engaging for students in kindergarten, but it will challenge them to apply knowledge and skills acquired

Score 4.0	In addition to score 3.0 performance, the student demonstrates in-depth inferences and applications that go beyond what was taught.
Score 3.0	The student will write grade-appropriate informative or explanatory texts to examine a topic and convey ideas, concepts, and information through the selection, organization, and analysis of relevant content. (W.6.2)
	The student will introduce a topic and organize ideas, concepts, and information using strategies such as definition, classification, comparison and contrast, and cause and effect. The student will include formatting (for example, headings), graphics, (for example, charts and tables), and multimedia when useful to aid comprehension. (W.6.2a)
	The student will develop the topic with relevant facts, definitions, concrete details, quotations, or other information and examples. (W.6.2b)
	The student will use appropriate transitions to clarify the relationships among ideas and concepts. (W.6.2c)
	The student will use precise language and domain-specific vocabulary to inform about or explain the topic. (W.6.2d)
	The student will establish and maintain a formal style. (W.6.2e)
	The student will provide a concluding statement or section that follows from the information or explanation presented. (W.6.2f)
Score 2.0	The student will recognize or recall specific vocabulary such as *analysis, cause and effect, chart, classification, comparison and contrast, comprehension, concluding statement, concrete, convey, definition, detail, domain-specific vocabulary, example, explain, fact, formal style, formatting, graphic, heading, idea, inform, informative or explanatory, introduce, multimedia, organization, organize, precise, quotation, relationship, relevant, selection, strategy, table, topic,* and *transition.*
	The student will perform basic processes, such as:
	• Identify the characteristics of a model informative or explanatory piece
	• Generate a list of details from relevant information related to the topic
	• Write informative or explanatory pieces using a teacher-provided template
Score 1.0	With help, partial success at score 2.0 content and score 3.0 content
Score 0.0	Even with help, no success

Source: Marzano et al., 2013, pp. 133–135.

Figure 2.11: Proficiency scale for writing explanatory texts, grade 6 ELA.

in earlier instruction, one of the hallmarks of performance assessment. The design of the performance assessment will provide the teacher with information about students' abilities on the academic standards to which it is aligned:

- Represent addition and subtraction in a variety of ways (with objects, fingers, mental images, drawings, sounds, acting out situations, verbal explanations, expressions, or equations) (MA10-GR.K-S.1-GLE.2-EO.a.i)

- Solve addition and subtraction word problems by adding and subtracting within 10 (MA10-GR.K-S.1-GLE.2-EO.a.ii)

- Model and solve addition and subtraction problems within the number 10 using objects such as coins and drawings (MA10-GR.K-S.1-GLE.2-EO.a.v; Colorado Department of Education, n.d.c)

The teacher can decide how much instructional time to devote to the performance assessment, what materials students will require, and how to present the assessment to students in a developmentally appropriate manner. But the students who create these mathematics books will be highly engaged and thinking deeply.

Summary

This chapter focuses on classroom assessment as a key part of the instructional cycle. Teachers should assess students frequently throughout the unit on content the class has recently learned. This allows them to respond quickly to misunderstandings and learning gaps to ensure all students master the standards. In particular, three key phases of assessment are (1) preassessments, (2) checks for understanding, and (3) end-of-cycle assessments. Assessments during all these phases of learning can take a variety of formats, including selected response, constructed response, discussions, and performance tasks. With this concrete information about types of classroom assessments in mind, the next chapter discusses collaborative practices that can improve the quality and consistency of individual assessments and educators' use of assessment to guide teaching and learning.

Chapter 2 Reflection Questions

1. What content should teachers assess during an instructional cycle?

2. What are the three key phases of assessment during an instructional cycle? Define each one.

3. Which level or levels of a proficiency scale are selected-response items most useful for assessing? Why?

4. How do discussions with students serve as assessments?

5. Thinking of a unit you have taught or currently teach, how might you apply the concepts or strategies discussed in this chapter?

3

Assessment Practices for Consistency and Collaboration

Key idea: Consistency is key when it comes to assessments. Whether you are an individual teacher or a collaborative team, you can improve the quality and consistency of your assessment practice with tools such as common assessments, assessment blueprints, and guidelines for administration and scoring.

Teachers need to know not only how to create high-quality classroom assessments, but also how to use the data they generate. Educational evaluation expert W. James Popham (2002) proclaimed that, "Our chief concern should be determining the quantity and quality of what students have learned" (p. 19). Without such emphasis, it is virtually impossible for teachers to know whether students are learning what is important for them to learn. This is true in a standards-based classroom as well; assessment must measure what students know and are able to do as defined by the standards taught in class. However, the idea of developing assessments can feel overwhelming to classroom teachers. Sometimes this is because they lack expertise on creating high-quality assessments. In fact, educators' perception is that they do not receive adequate assessment training during their preservice teacher preparation programs. According to the National Council on Teacher Quality, teacher training does not sufficiently prepare future teachers to assess students; 80 percent of surveyed teachers felt that their coursework inadequately addressed assessment literacy (Greenberg & Walsh, 2012). Education research and assessment expert Cynthia Campbell (2013) agreed when she said, "Research investigating evaluation practices of classroom teachers has consistently reported concerns about the adequacy of their assessment knowledge and skill" (p. 71).

While it is obviously important for teachers to understand the purposes and types of assessments as well as their role in the instructional cycle, an often-overlooked aspect of assessment literacy is this: teacher collaboration improves effective assessment practices. A survey of educators by the National Center for Literacy Education (NCLE, 2013) found that respondents cited an increase in teacher ability to use student data as a product of teacher collaboration. Collaborative teams such as those organized within a professional learning community (PLC) offer teachers the opportunity to establish shared visions of curriculum, clear instructional goals, and comprehensive schoolwide or districtwide systems for evaluating and reporting student performance (DuFour, DuFour, Eaker, Mattos, & Muhammad, 2021; Wolf, 1993). In this chapter, we explore practices that teachers can employ to ensure high-quality assessment development and use. These include:

- Common assessments
- Existing common and individual assessments
- Assessment blueprints
- Assessment item frameworks
- Common assessment administration guidance
- Scoring guidance
- Data protocols

Each of these practices helps teachers assess students consistently—both for individual teachers assessing numerous students and classes and for collaborative teams of teachers who instruct the same content. In the standards-based classroom, observing such practices increases the applicability and worth of the assessment data, providing teachers and their students with accurate information about the learning that has occurred related to the standards.

Common Assessments

The most basic collaborative assessment practice is the use of common assessments. A *common assessment* is one that is selected or developed and administered by multiple teachers who teach the same content area and grade level or course. In standards-based learning, colleagues who teach the same classes or grade level address the same standards and associated proficiency scales and can therefore develop and use the same assessments. This provides the unique opportunity to compare assessment data across classrooms.

The development and use of various assessment types remain the same when using them as common assessments, but there are specific considerations that emerge when multiple teachers give the same assessment. From the outset, the team of teachers should discuss and agree on the purpose, design, and administration of a common assessment. A common purpose will help align not only the design of the assessment but also when the assessment is given during an instructional cycle. Determining a common purpose, collaborating on the design, and agreeing on when and how to administer the assessment ensure that the teachers can compare the results. Proficiency scales provide the common language about learning goals and expectations across classrooms, and consistency in assessment design and administration makes it more likely that variation in the data between classrooms results from differences in instruction, which teachers can analyze collaboratively for the benefit of all students.

One advantage of common assessment is the ability for teachers to analyze the data from the assessment as a team. After the assessment takes place, the team of teachers can look at student performance for each test item or element of the rubric and discuss performance across all the classes in which the assessment was given. This provides insight about the effectiveness of each aspect of instruction. We discuss this process in more depth later in this chapter (see Data Protocols, page 63). It may identify a specific learning target that the entire team needs to reteach or an area where certain classes need additional instruction. Teachers can access the expertise of the rest of the team in designing a plan for reteaching.

Although individual teachers often use performance assessments in their classrooms, these can also serve as common assessments. There are situations where a common performance assessment makes sense and others where it is likely inappropriate. In content areas centered on performance rather than factual knowledge, such as the performing arts, visual arts, physical education, and so on, common performance assessments will occur regularly. While traditional academic content areas might make less frequent use of common performance assessments, teams of teachers will likely identify situations where they are appropriate. For example, a science team might design a common performance assessment around a lab procedure. The situation and the needs of the team of teachers will dictate whether a common performance assessment is appropriate.

Let's consider a common performance assessment that might be given at the sixth-grade level in physical education.

Sixth-Grade PE Dance Project

Ohio Physical Education Learning Standards

Standard 1: Demonstrate competency in a variety of motor skills and movement patterns.

Benchmark A: Demonstrate movement skills and patterns in a variety of individual performance activities and lifetime physical activities.

Prompt: You will be creating a dance video similar to your very own TikTok!

Requirements:

1. You will create an original dance video lasting thirty seconds to one minute.

2. Your routine must include both arm and leg movements.

3. You will choose a school-appropriate song for your routine and video.

4. Once you have mastered your routine (practiced and know it well), you will record yourself performing with the music and then upload that video to Google Classroom or my school email account.

5. Follow the rubric to earn that top score!

6. Your completed video is due to me on or before Friday, March 19 during class period.

Source for standard: Ohio Department of Education, 2020.

Source: © 2022 by Tabitha Merideth. Adapted with permission.

Note that the assessment is aligned to the state standard and benchmark. The state requirements at sixth grade include a focus on developing movement and coordination; one method to do this is dance. Figure 3.1 is the rubric students receive. The rubric gives details about teacher expectations so the students know the expectations prior to designing the dance, rehearsing, and recording the performance. In creating this rubric, the team of teachers who will give this assessment carefully discuss expectations for the assessment as well as what successful performance looks like. The shared rubric allows the teachers to score students consistently. Note that the common assessment task and rubric would easily function as an individual teacher's performance assessment just as well as a common performance assessment.

	Developing—Score 1.0	Progressing—Score 2.0	Satisfactory—Score 3.0	Excellent—Score 4.0
Rhythm and Tempo The dancer demonstrates ability to stay in time with the music.	In attempting to establish and maintain a rhythm, the dancer often does not align with the beat of the music.	In attempting to establish and maintain a rhythm, the dancer clearly understands the tempo but occasionally makes errors in rhythm.	Solid understanding of rhythm and tempo demonstrated by rarely making errors in rhythm.	Outstanding accuracy in maintaining beat, tempo, and rhythm in the dance performance.
Preparedness The dance is well rehearsed.	Performance shows little evidence of preparation.	Dancer seems unprepared and there is evidence of insufficient rehearsal. Many dance moves appear uncertain or are missed entirely.	Dance preparation is adequate but the performance would have benefited from additional rehearsal. Some dance moves are uncertain or missed.	Performance is polished through sufficient rehearsal. Dance moves are well performed and assured.
Enthusiasm The dancer demonstrates involvement in the emotion or mood of the dance.	Little interest in the performance is demonstrated.	Dancer uses body language and facial expressions occasionally to generate emotions.	Dancer often uses facial expressions and body language to generate interest and enthusiasm.	Facial expressions and body language are extensively integrated into the performance to generate a strong interest and enthusiasm.
Creativity in Choreography The dance moves chosen display a certain level of creativity.	Performance shows little or no creativity.	Dancer performs basic dance moves.	Dancer has added one to two complex dance moves.	Dancer has integrated many complex dance moves into the performance.

Source: © 2022 by Tabitha Merideth. Adapted with permission.

Figure 3.1: Rubric for dance project performance, grade 6 PE.

Existing Common and Individual Assessments

While shifting toward standards-based learning or adopting collaborative assessment practices might be new, it is not necessary to start completely from scratch. We suggest that teachers begin by examining existing assessments to align them to the priority standards and proficiency scales. Heflebower and colleagues (2014) referred to this practice as *backmapping* and offered four steps for completing the backmapping process:

1. Teachers identify the proficiency scale or scales that need to be measured by the existing assessment.
2. Teachers examine each assessment item to determine the level of the proficiency scale that it corresponds with and label it appropriately.
3. Teachers identify assessment items that do not correspond to any levels of the proficiency scale and remove them.
4. Teachers add items for levels of the proficiency scale not represented by items already on the assessment. (p. 47)

When a teacher or team of teachers begins with existing assessments, the amount of work that needs to occur is less overwhelming. It also honors previous assessment work and affirms the time, energy, and effort educators expended. As an example, suppose a team of sixth-grade mathematics teachers unpacked a particular priority standard as follows.

The student will write, read, and evaluate expressions in which letters stand for numbers.

- Write, read, and evaluate expressions with variables.

- Recognize important academic vocabulary, such as *coefficient, constant, difference, evaluate, express, factor, product, quotient, sum, term,* and *variable.*

- Read and write expressions with variables.

- Evaluate expressions with variables.

- Use the order of operations to evaluate algebraic expressions and formulas in real-world problems.

This content is not new to the sixth-grade learning environment; the teachers taught and administered assessments on this topic before adopting standards-based learning. When examining their existing assessments, teachers will find items or tasks that align closely to the learning targets on this proficiency scale. Imagine that this team has the following item on an existing assessment.

The expression $c + 0.07c$ can be used to find the total cost of an item with 7 percent sales tax, where c is the pretax cost of the item. Use the expression to find the total cost of an item that costs $25.

The team might choose to reuse this item on a new common assessment because it aligns tightly to the learning target, "Evaluate expressions with variables." Because of the close alignment to the learning target on the proficiency scale, teachers will have important information about each student's understanding following the use of this item.

Assessment Blueprints

While proficiency scales provide a structure that informs the development of individual classroom assessments, it is also important to have a deliberate plan for the use of assessments relative to a specific topic or standard. An *assessment blueprint* includes the assessments that students will receive, the purpose of each assessment, and potential instructional reactions based on that assessment data. In a standards-based classroom, teachers will want to assess specific learning targets for a specific standard. These learning targets are defined in the proficiency scale and an assessment blueprint allows teachers to directly plan which levels of the scale and which specific learning targets they will include in any specific assessment. This is an important step to creating aligned assessments that generate data that teachers can use to inform instructional decisions. Consider the function of a blueprint for a building. It allows builders to replicate the same building multiple times in different locations. At the same time, it also allows for adaptations when they are desired or needed. Likewise, teachers can replicate a classroom assessment blueprint across multiple measurement topics or standards and still allow for adaptations when necessary. A blueprint might specify what content or scale levels to assess, the purpose of each assessment, and the actions that might occur based on the assessment results. However, the assessment blueprint does not need to identify specific types of assessment, allowing teachers and teams to remain flexible based on the content and students' needs.

The concept of an assessment blueprint is especially important for collaborative teams that are using common assessments. A collaborative team should identify which specific assessments in the sequence will be common assessments and collaborate on the development of those. As teams focus on developing the common assessments, they consult the scales, identify types of assessments, and collaboratively design specific assessment items or tasks based on the intended learning.

An example of a classroom assessment blueprint appears in figure 3.2. The example shows how an assessment blueprint lays out a series of assessments that inform teachers and students about where they are in their progression of learning and identifies possible teaching reactions to the assessment results.

An assessment blueprint should be easily applicable across different topics or standards. It should also provide time and opportunities for teachers to use additional assessment strategies with the whole class or individual students when they see the need to do so. For example, assume several students do well on the third assessment from the example blueprint. The teacher might choose to use a probing discussion to determine whether each of those students is proficient and ready to work toward score 4.0 content.

Likewise, a good assessment blueprint does not identify specific types of assessments teachers will use. Rather, teachers make such decisions at their discretion as they apply the blueprint to different topics, standards, and learning situations. In a specific ELA instructional cycle, the second assessment recommended by the example blueprint might involve students' writing a short paragraph about a specific topic; in a subsequent unit on

Assessments	Purposes and Potential Actions
Assessment 1 Preassessment of score 2.0 concepts Possibly include some level 3.0 opportunities to assess for existing proficiency	Identify initial gaps in foundational knowledge and skills that may need to be reviewed or retaught during initial instruction. Look for existing proficiency and consider individual assessments. Have students begin individual progress tracking.
Assessment 2 Reassessment of key foundational skills and assessment of any score 3.0 content taught to this point	Identify and correct the most common errors and misunderstandings in early learning for this concept. Identify students who grasp the content quickly or possibly already know it. Students track individual progress.
Assessment 3 Mid-unit assessment of proficiency score 3.0 concepts	Celebrate successful demonstrations of proficient level knowledge with the whole class or individually. Identify common misunderstandings and initiate reteaching of those concepts, if necessary. Identify students moving ahead quickly who are ready for score 4.0 work. Students track individual progress.
Assessment 4 Second assessment of proficiency score 3.0 concepts	Recognize and celebrate whole class and individual student growth. Look for improvement in areas of misunderstanding that were retaught previously. Conduct one-on-one conferences to further assess students' learning as needed. Identify clearly proficient students and move them to level 4. Students track individual progress.
Assessment 5 End-of-cycle assessment with main focus on score 3.0 proficiency Score 4.0 assessment options for students who are ready	Measure status and growth in the content for all students. Look for elimination of misunderstandings that occurred early in the unit. Consider extended time for reteaching and additional assessment opportunities if needed.

Figure 3.2: Sample classroom assessment blueprint.

a different topic (still guided by the same assessment blueprint), the second assessment might involve students' developing a storyboard based on their interpretations of a short story. The purpose of the assessments is the same as identified in the assessment blueprint, but the type of assessment is different because the content in each proficiency scale is different and needs to be measured appropriately.

In addition to the assessment blueprint's direction regarding assessment throughout the instructional cycle, teachers can also develop guidance on how to assess students at different levels of the proficiency scale. Figure 3.3 (page 58) provides an example of a document that gives suggestions for assessment approaches at each level of the proficiency scale. A teacher wishing to create an assessment of student learning at scores 2.0, 3.0, and 4.0 on the proficiency scale might look through this chart and select one suggestion at each level as a starting point for the creation of an aligned assessment. Note that the tasks listed at each level differ since student learning will differ at each level. In this way, a teacher can provide the appropriate level of challenge for evaluating student learning at each level of the scale.

Score 4.0	
In score 4.0 assessments, students apply the knowledge and skills from score 3.0. These assessments typically involves self-directed exploration and application of the content. Consider offering a choice in assessment tasks in this phase.	• Use problem-based learning approaches whenever appropriate. Offer choices in these tasks whenever possible. • Develop tasks that require the use of the cumulative knowledge and skills within the scale. • As part of these assessments, have students identify sources of their knowledge and information that support their thinking and actions. • Require students to defend positions contrary to their own if this type of task is appropriate. • Use probing discussions with students to assess the depth of their understanding at this level. • Consider assessment opportunities at this level that could engage the entire class in this level of thinking when appropriate.
Score 3.0 Score 3.0 assessments consist of questions and tasks at the level of proficiency. Use these over several sessions to allow all learners an opportunity to understand and perform at this level.	• Develop three to five questions or tasks that you can use to accurately assess early proficiency in this level of rigor. • Consider groups of students working together initially. (Assess small groups and correct common errors within the groups or across the whole class. Celebrate and affirm correct thinking.) • Develop an additional set of questions or tasks at this level of rigor. Use these to assess individual proficiency. Look for elimination of prior errors in performance. • Identify learners possibly ready for score 4.0 and learners with knowledge or skill gaps that need to be addressed.
Score 2.0 Score 2.0 assessments assess foundational understandings. Ask and re-ask these questions to assess acquisition of foundational knowledge during the first few lessons.	• Students self-assess their knowledge of content vocabulary and elaborate on any terms they think they might already know. • Preassess student knowledge with oral questions to the whole class or small groups. Select several foundational learning targets to develop these questions. (Based on this assessment data, teach or review key concepts in which there are large gaps of understanding.) • Ask students to perform basic skills or tasks at this level. Use a data recording form to score individual students and class performance on these skills. (Identify the most common errors and address them as immediately as possible.) • Prepare a few scale score 3.0 content questions to use as part of the preassessment. Use them in the preassessment if learners are ready for this challenge.

Figure 3.3: Assessment guide based on proficiency scales.

Assessment Item Frameworks

Just as assessment blueprints provide a consistent framework for assessments throughout an instructional cycle, teachers can also use *item frameworks* to design individual assessment items. These are commonly used types of assessment questions within specific content areas (Marzano et al., 2022). The basic structures indicated by various item frameworks aid teachers in generating test questions for different types of content. Use of such item frameworks aligns with one of the central tenets of standards-based learning: student instruction and assessment should be specifically coordinated with the intellectual requirements found in the standards. These requirements often vary from content area to content area, so the use of frameworks aligned to content areas helps teachers meet this basic need. Robert J. Marzano, Christopher W. Dodson, Julia A. Simms, and Jacob P. Wipf (2022) provided item frames for ELA, mathematics, and science based on analyses of large-scale assessments. Using such item frames when developing classroom assessments has the dual benefits of improving assessment quality and familiarizing students with the types of questions they are likely to encounter on state exams (Marzano et al., 2022).

Common structures in ELA assessments include a number of *frames* that vary according to the relationship between pieces of information that the question is asking about. For example, short constructed-response items that follow the *evidence frame* typically ask students to read two or more passages and identify which one provides stronger support for a given claim (Marzano et al., 2022). Teachers can follow this simple process to create an assessment item using the evidence frame:

1. Select two or more texts on the same topic, with one text clearly focusing on a specific facet of the topic.

2. Write an item using the following stem.

    - Which source is most helpful or relevant?

3. Add a prompt for evidence such as:

    - Support your answer with details from the text.

    - Use details from the text to support your answer.

    - Use two details from the source to support your explanation. (Marzano et al., 2022, p. 49)

The following item is the outcome of using these three steps.

Carefully read *Importance of Recycling* and *Reusing Trash?* Then answer the following question.

Which source is the most helpful or relevant? Support your answer with details from the text.

Common structures in mathematics assessments fall into categories of specific mathematics content, such as geometry, measurement, or operations. The complexity of content changes with the grade level. For example, within the category of geometry, third graders might be learning about two-dimensional and three-dimensional shapes. A simple selected-response item framework for this category asks students to correctly identify a certain type of shape (for example, squares, hexagons, or triangles) from a set (Marzano et al., 2022).

Finally, it is important to note that teachers can directly communicate item frameworks to students (Marzano et al., 2022). Direct instruction increases their familiarity with common item frameworks that they will encounter on tests. Students will be better able to demonstrate their knowledge on different types of assessment items if they can recognize and develop mental models for those different types. When planning to teach students about the structure of assessment questions, teachers can consider what features of the item they need to point out to students, the thought process for answering the question, and the academic content or skills required to answer it. To access item frameworks for ELA, mathematics, and science, consult *Ethical Test Preparation in the Classroom* (Marzano et al., 2022).

Common Assessment Administration Guidance

Collaborative teams should not only use common assessments but also administer those common assessments in a consistent manner, especially when it comes to end-of-cycle assessments. When creating an assessment, teachers should also consider how to present it to students, including the time period in which the common assessment must be given, the length of time students will have to complete the assessment, and special considerations regarding the way in which the assessment is discussed, the verbal directions provided, and any resources students will be allowed to use during the assessment. This planning process results in a document for each common assessment called *administration guidance*. It ensures that students in different classes have a similar test experience so that educators are better able to compare the resulting data between teachers or sections of a course. In a standards-based environment, this practice is key to creating consistency between classrooms so all students have equal opportunities to master the priority standards. The following is an example of assessment guidance for a seventh-grade ELA end-of-cycle assessment on citing evidence.

> - Allow two class periods for the administration of this assessment. Teachers may divide the assessment in any manner of their choosing.
>
> - Go over the directions on each part of the assessment with the entire class. Be sure to emphasize that students only need to complete two of the three score 3.0 items and one of the two score 4.0 items.
>
> - The teacher may support students with reading the questions on the assessment; however, students must read the passage of text independently. It is also acceptable to clarify directions for students as needed.

Teachers should treat performance assessments in a similar manner when creating administration guidance. Recall the sixth-grade PE dance assignment from earlier in the chapter (page 53). Administration guidance for that assessment might read as follows.

> - Assessment assigned within the week of October 5.
> - Teacher reads directions aloud to students and explains details.
> - Students will have twenty minutes of class time each period for one week to work on the assessment individually.
> - Assessment is due one week after it is assigned.

While administration of performance assessments is essentially similar to the administration of other types of classroom assessments, teachers should address some considerations before providing students with the prompt for the assessment.

- Is the assessment given in isolation, by a single teacher, or will multiple teachers give the same assessment (common assessment)?

- What is a reasonable amount of time (both in class and out of class) for students to adequately prepare for their assessment?

- How will the in-class time be structured?

- What will teachers accept as a proficient performance?

- How will teachers judge the performance? Will only the teacher score it, or will other students do peer evaluations? In the case of peer evaluations, how will the teacher ensure they are effective but nonthreatening? What role (if any) will peer evaluation have in the performer's overall score?

- How will teachers share feedback on the performance with students?

Administration guidance is extremely helpful when multiple teachers give a common assessment, as it guarantees that the assessment and practices associated with it are indeed common. All teachers should hold themselves accountable to exercising the administration guidance with fidelity. When administration differs across teachers, there is just cause for concern regarding fairness. Consider the preceding example administration guidance, which states that the teacher should read the directions to students. Imagine two classrooms, where teacher A spends considerable time going over the directions and answering students' questions, perhaps even asking students to highlight important words and phrases to ensure they pay attention. In comparison, teacher B lets students read the directions on their own with no follow-up. Which classroom of students has an advantage? Obviously, the students in teacher A's classroom will have a clearer and more thorough understanding of the assessment in front of them.

Single teachers also can and should make use of administration guidance. Teachers often give the same assessment to multiple sections, classes, or groups of students. This is especially true in secondary environments or departmentalized elementary schools. In these situations, the same teacher gives the same test on multiple occasions and must still make sure different groups of students experience a similar test administration. The administration guidance minimizes differences that may occur across these multiple test opportunities.

Scoring Guidance

After administering an assessment, the natural next step is to score that assessment. Just as planning for consistency in administration is necessary, it is also important to plan for consistency in the scoring process. Again, this consistency is of particular importance for end-of-cycle assessments, which often carry the most weight when determining students' summative scores. The primary question addressed through scoring guidance is, What level of student performance equates to mastery of the standard or standards included on this assessment? Scoring guidance minimizes subjectivity across scorers and makes it easier to exercise consistency when making decisions about students' level of performance relative to the standards.

Consider a sixth-grade science instructional cycle on the topic of reproduction. The end-of-cycle assessment is based on a proficiency scale and includes eight fill-in-the-blank items with a word bank for score 2.0, five constructed-response items (including two multipart items) for score 3.0, and one multipart extended constructed-response item for score 4.0.

The teacher or team needs to develop scoring guidance for this assessment so there is a shared understanding of what degree of performance equates to mastery of each level on the scale. For example, how many of the eight fill-in-the-blank items does a student need to answer correctly to be considered proficient with the score 2.0 content? In addition to degree of accuracy required, scoring guidance should offer information about the content of constructed-response items—perhaps a list of required elements or possible acceptable responses. Scoring guidance for a score 3.0 item that asks, "What are some advantages and disadvantages of cross-breeding plants or animals?" might consist of a teacher-generated list of advantages and disadvantages. Teachers refer to this list as they score this item on each student's assessment, helping to ensure consistency.

Figure 3.4 displays sample scoring guidance for the reproduction assessment. All teachers follow this agreed-on guidance to ensure they make similar decisions about student performance.

Score 4.0 performance	Student answers item correctly.
Score 3.0 performance	Student answers four or more items correctly, including the multipart items.
Score 2.0 performance	Student answers six or more items correctly.

Figure 3.4: Scoring guidance for reproduction assessment.

Another way to establish scoring guidance for constructed-response items is to use exemplars, or *anchors*. Teachers can select several student responses (perhaps a completely correct response, a partially correct response, and an incorrect response) to serve as anchors while scoring the remaining student responses. An alternative method is for teachers to take the assessment and draft exemplary responses to serve as anchors. As they score assessments, teachers compare each student's response to the anchors to help apply a consistent definition of a correct or complete answer.

Scoring guidance also applies to performance assessments. As with more traditional assessment items, exemplars play an important role in establishing criteria for each level of performance on the assessment. Teachers can create a bank of typical performance assessment responses and then use them as a basis for discussion, or *norming*, before scoring. For example, one of the authors of this book, Jeff, has served as a scorer for the College Board's Advanced Placement exams. When the test readers train to score open-ended response items (essays or other elaborate responses that require scoring judgment), they thoroughly review and discuss exemplars as a method to ensure all scorers have a consistent understanding of what should be present in a response at each level on the scoring rubric. Returning again to the sixth-grade PE dance assessment, scoring guidance might consist of the following.

- Scoring should follow the rubric provided to students.

- Teacher may confer with the student when clarifications are needed in order to make a decision about scoring.

- In certain cases, teachers may consult other members of the team about a scoring decision.

With performance assessments that take the form of a recording or an artifact (such as the dance video example, drama performances, music performance, or even presentations in core content classes), teachers can also use anchors for reference as they score student performances. A team of teachers could watch recordings or examine artifacts together after administering the assessment to select exemplars and ensure similar scoring, or they could select exemplars from prior administrations to serve as anchors. Teams can choose either option with each administration of a given assessment, providing flexibility.

When performance assessments are conducted live in class, it may not be possible for the team of teachers to review sample performances ahead of time to standardize their understanding of success. In this case, teachers should set and discuss clear, detailed scoring criteria in advance. For example, will all teachers score the quality of oral presentations on a common performance assessment or only the content of the presentation? Teachers must collectively decide how they will handle this before the live scoring takes place. A discussion of the scoring criteria, based solidly on a rubric and the proficiency scale for the performance assessment, is very important in meeting the goal of being as objective as possible and providing students with high-quality feedback on their work.

As with administration guidance, scoring guidance is just as useful to individual teachers as it is to collaborative teams. Most classroom teachers' schedules prevent scoring assessments in a single sitting. For example, a teacher may have fifteen minutes to work on scoring assessments prior to students arriving in the morning. Later in the day, another twenty minutes are available over lunch period. During prep period, the teacher may be able to score a few more assessments. The point is that it is difficult to maintain consistency when scoring is distributed intermittently over the course of a day or two. In the end, scoring guidance helps teachers grade different students' work fairly.

Data Protocols

The final collaborative assessment practice we discuss in this chapter is the data protocol. This is a method of reviewing and discussing assessment results to make instructional decisions. When collaborative teams give common assessments, they should use a data protocol to discuss the results. Using a data protocol for any common assessment provides a structure for the careful review of each aspect of the assessment and as a way to determine how the data from the assessment will be used. In the standards-based classroom, a data protocol helps ensure that teachers use assessment results to improve student progress in the learning progression of the proficiency scale.

One version of a data protocol is to break down student performance on each assessment item, discuss the results, and record any suspected reasons for notably high or low performance, plans for further instruction, or other notes. Figure 3.5 shows a sample data protocol for a five-question quiz on score 2.0 and score 3.0 content from a particular proficiency scale. The teachers have taken notes based on their discussions of how students performed on each item.

Assessment Item	Scale Level	Performance Percentages	Notes
1	2.0	Correct: 85 percent Partially correct: 15 percent Incorrect: 0 percent	The percentage of students showing mastery of this concept increased by thirty-five points from the preassessment.
2	2.0	Correct: 90 percent Partially correct: 5 percent Incorrect: 0 percent	Students scoring partially correct made silly mistakes, prompting no concerns.
3	3.0	Correct: 60 percent Partially correct: 10 percent Incorrect: 30 percent	Students scoring partially correct or incorrect all struggled with the initial steps in the process, which affected the end result.
4	3.0	Correct: 50 percent Partially correct: 20 percent Incorrect: 30 percent	Half of students struggled; we should consider reteaching this concept.
5	3.0	Correct: 12 percent Partially correct: 2 percent Incorrect: 80 percent	We have only covered this one time in class. These results make sense at this point.

Figure 3.5: Sample data protocol with performance percentages for each item.

*Visit **MarzanoResources.com/reproducibles** for a blank reproducible version of this figure.*

Data protocols can also operate on a more holistic level. This can help teachers discuss the quality of the assessment itself and make decisions about where to go next in the instructional cycle or how to group students according to need. Figure 3.6 is a sample data protocol that includes questions we believe are important for teachers to answer in relation to an end-of-cycle assessment or any assessment for which a team of teachers wants to engage in a thorough review.

We recommend that a teacher or team of teachers adopt or develop a data protocol and use it consistently throughout the year. When teachers analyze data in this way, planning next steps for instruction is easier and typically better meets the needs of students. The information gleaned from the data allows teachers to group students and teach lessons responsively based on current levels of performance. We discuss using data from assessments in more detail in chapter 6 (page 103).

Assessment Data Protocol	Notes
1. On which parts of the assessment did students perform well? Why do we believe this is the case?	Students performed well on questions 1–5, 7, and 9–10. This aligns with the indications from classwork prior to the assessment. Students in class appeared to know the material well and the assessment provided additional specific data that this was the case.
2. On which parts of the assessment did students struggle? Why do we believe this is the case?	Students did not perform well on questions 6 and 8. We believe question 6 was written in a confusing way. Question 8 indicates a learning target that needs additional and perhaps differentiated reteaching.
3. Do we need to revise any assessment items? Which items? Why?	Nearly all students missed question 6. We should revise the question for clarity.
4. Which students are in need of special attention?	Additional opportunity to learn: Brian, Sean, Lindsey, Pedro, Karen Additional practicing and deepening: All students not listed above or below Enrichment: Andy, Aisha, Kyle, Ian, Hope, Jennifer, Mike, Marcel, Bobby
5. Are there other important findings about this common assessment that we need to record?	The administration of this assessment went pretty well, but we think we should increase the amount of time planned for the administration by about ten to fifteen minutes.
Action steps resulting from the data:	1. Revise assessment item 6. 2. Design interventions for students identified in step 4. 3. Revise administration guidance to give students ten to fifteen more minutes for this assessment.

Source: Adapted from Marzano et al., 2016.

Figure 3.6: Sample data protocol for holistic review of an assessment.

*Visit **MarzanoResources.com/reproducibles** for a blank reproducible version of this figure.*

Summary

In this chapter, we discussed practices that help teachers and teams design, administer, and score assessments consistently. Collaborative teams should create and administer common assessments, which can be formative checks for understanding or end-of-cycle assessments. We also recommended that teachers and teams shifting to standards-based learning make use of existing assessments to lighten their load. When planning an instructional cycle, educators should create an assessment blueprint to clarify at what points during the cycle they will assess various content. For developing individual assessments, assessment item frames can help teachers write high-quality questions and tasks that also familiarize students with common types of test questions. Two additional components of classroom assessment are administration guidance and scoring guidance. These two components ensure that adequate planning goes into how the assessment is given and how it will be scored, for the sake of consistency. Finally, data protocols guide teachers as they discuss assessment results and make instructional decisions accordingly. The tools described in this chapter are essential for any assessment administered and scored by multiple teachers, but they are also helpful to an individual teacher.

Chapter 3 Reflection Questions

1. How can a teacher or team of teachers use existing classroom assessments within a newly developed instructional cycle?

2. What is the role of the assessment blueprint in the instructional cycle? What information does it contain? What information does it not specify?

3. What are assessment item frameworks and how might teachers use them to develop classroom assessments?

4. What is the purpose of a data protocol?

5. Thinking of a unit you have taught or currently teach, how might you apply the concepts or strategies discussed in this chapter?

4 Technical Quality

Key idea: To trust the results of classroom assessments, educators need to ensure assessments and scoring processes function in valid, reliable, and fair ways, and that they can be accurately interpreted in terms of mastery levels.

While the previous chapter discussed some practical and collaborative approaches to making assessments more consistent, this chapter reviews the technical aspects of what makes assessments high quality. In a standards-based learning environment, teachers gather information about student learning throughout an instructional cycle. They need relevant, timely, and trustworthy information about their students. Because teachers examine assessments carefully for the sake of making important instructional decisions, it is paramount that these tools are high quality. If quality is lacking, the information teachers glean may be invalid, inaccurate, unreliable, and even misleading, increasing the potential for making poor judgments about student performance. Garbage in, garbage out, as the adage goes. All assessments, and especially end-of-cycle assessments, must be technically sound.

It is important to mention at the beginning of this chapter that while it includes valuable assessment information for educators, some of the content might feel quite specialized—even a bit outside the realm of a classroom teacher. However, we strongly believe that understanding the technical design of a high-quality classroom assessment (especially end-of-cycle assessments) is paramount for today's teachers. As Gareis and Grant (2008) explained:

> Simply put, teachers must come to consider their assessment practices as integral to their instructional practices. And, just as most teachers recognize that positive regard, engagement, and relevancy are doorways to student learning, so too, must teachers realize that their assessment practices should be engaging, fair, and relevant as well. (pp. 40–41)

Given how dramatically assessment results can affect students, we urge classroom teachers to expand their technical knowledge of this topic. In larger systems, it is possible that building- or district-level personnel create, monitor, and provide the administrative guidance for assessments. In others, these actions are the responsibility of grade-level teams or other collaborative teams. In all cases, foundational knowledge of high-quality classroom assessments will help teachers not only understand them better but also trust the results when using them in a standards-based learning environment.

This chapter addresses four principles to help resolve unintentional deficits in assessment quality: (1) validity, (2) fairness, (3) reliability, and (4) appropriate mastery levels (Buckendahl, Impara, & Plake, 2002; Heflebower, 2009; Heflebower et al., 2021; Marzano et al., 2022; Nebraska Department of Education [NDE], 2007; Stiggins, 1995; Stiggins & Chappuis, 2012). We define these four criteria briefly as follows.

1. **Validity:** The classroom assessment is aligned to the state or provincial standards and there is sufficient coverage to adequately determine proficiency.

2. **Fairness:** The classroom assessment is unbiased, appropriately challenging, and occurs after students have had the opportunity to learn the content.

3. **Reliability:** The classroom assessment produces consistent, accurate results, and the teacher uses proven strategies to check the reliability of objectively and subjectively scored assessments.

4. **Appropriate mastery levels:** The classroom assessment is scored according to definite criteria for mastery. Proficiency is not arbitrarily assigned (NDE, 2002).

These criteria represent sound characteristics of quality assessments defined by the Standards for Educational and Psychological Testing (American Educational Research Association, American Psychological Association, & National Council on Measurement in Education, 1999, 2014), as well as the Nebraska Department of Education (2007) in conjunction with the Buros Center for Testing (http://buros.org). In a standards-based learning environment, teachers must be certain that assessments align with the standards taught, that assessment design is fair, that scoring practices are reliable and consistent across classrooms, and that scoring decisions accurately reflect criteria for mastery. Figure 4.1 displays a checklist that addresses the technical quality components of validity, fairness, reliability, and appropriate mastery levels. Teachers can use this tool to gain confidence about the quality of their classroom assessments, and teams of teachers can use it during collaborative team meetings to review common assessments for technical quality. If teachers indicate *no* for any of the criteria, they should generate actionable suggestions for how to improve specific items or the assessment overall and then make those revisions. Visit **MarzanoResources.com/reproducibles** for additional tools for checking the technical quality of assessments.

The remainder of this chapter goes into detail about validity, fairness, reliability, and appropriate mastery levels. While these components might initially appear complex and challenging, we provide practical options for classroom teachers' use.

Content area or course: _____ Grade level: _____

Standards: _____

Technical Quality Component	Review Criteria	Yes	No	Assessment Items That Need Revision	Suggestions for Revision
Validity	The assessment measures the knowledge and skills in the standards.				
Validity	Assessment items or tasks align to the verbiage in the learning targets on the proficiency scale.				
Fairness	Students have had the opportunity to learn the content on the assessment.				
Fairness	Directions for students are present, clear, and concise.				
Fairness	The assessment is written at the appropriate reading level.				
Fairness	The assessment is free from bias.				
Reliability	Administration guidance for teachers is present, clear, and concise.				
Reliability	A rubric, scoring criteria, or checklist is present for constructed-response and performance items.				
Appropriate Mastery Levels	Cut scores are set using a robust process.				

Figure 4.1: Checklist for assessment technical quality.

Visit MarzanoResources.com/reproducibles for a free reproducible version of this figure.

Ensuring Valid Classroom Assessments

Validity, in simple terms, means that the classroom assessment provides the information that the teacher is looking for. As Gareis and Grant (2008) defined it, "Validity is concerned with whether a test, quiz, project, or performance assesses what we intend it to assess" (p. 34). Many assessment experts categorize validity into a few types (Brookhart, 2012; Gareis & Grant, 2015, Marzano, 2018; Popham, 2017), including *construct validity*, *content validity*, *criterion validity*, and *consequential validity*. A classroom teacher need not master these concepts to ensure classroom assessments are valid, but a brief description will establish background knowledge.

- **Construct validity:** How accurately does a classroom assessment align with the priority standards or learning targets? Does it match the level of cognitive demand? If a standard indicates students must be able to explain a concept, then associated assessment items must ask students to actually explain the concept, not simply select the best explanation offered.

- **Content validity:** How adequately does the classroom assessment sample content from the standards or learning targets? Are there enough items related to a specific learning target to draw a solid conclusion about students' understanding of it? Two true-or-false items, for example, would likely not be sufficient to establish a student's level of knowledge on a particular skill.

- **Criterion validity:** Does a newly developed assessment have a mathematical correlation to an established highly valid assessment? As Marzano (2018) stated, "To establish criterion-related validity for an assessment . . . a researcher typically computes a correlation coefficient between the newly developed test and some other assessment considered to already be a valid measure of the topic" (p. 18). This type of validity is important in the technical literature, but it is not often present in classroom teachers' assessment practices.

- **Consequential validity:** How does the teacher interpret the data from assessments to gauge a student's knowledge, skill, and understanding? Should the teacher refer a student to intervention, honors programs, early promotion, special education, or similar? Are these assessment data strong enough to inform such a decision? This is important for the classroom teacher to consider. Using assessment data appropriately is key.

While these categories of validity are important, teachers do not need to reach perfection to improve their assessment practices. Gareis and Grant (2008) said:

> Rarely is a test either perfectly valid or perfectly invalid. Validity is usually a question of degree. . . . Therefore when contemplating and discussing the validity of an assessment, it is best to use relative terms, such as *high validity, moderate validity*, and *low validity*. (p. 34)

The following sections present two helpful practices for ensuring that an assessment's degree of validity is high.

Aligning Assessment Items to Learning Targets

As we describe throughout this book, assessment items should be aligned to particular learning targets or levels of proficiency scales. Consider the example in figure 4.2, which is a set of assessment items for eighth-grade civics. The levels of the associated proficiency scale are noted next to each group of assessment items to show the clear differences in complexity. This is how proficiency scales help inform validity, and in turn, assessments measure the intended learning expressed in the different levels of the scale.

Score 2.0	1.	What is the agreement between people and their government proposed by Rousseau?
		a. Constitution c. Social arrangement
		b. Declaration of Independence d. Social contract
	2.	What was the addition to the Constitution that guaranteed personal freedoms?
		a. Bill of Rights c. Freedom of religion
		b. Declaration of Independence d. Social contract
	3.	What document espoused the core values of life, liberty, and the pursuit of happiness?
		a. Bill of Rights c. Declaration of Independence
		b. Constitution d. Tenth Amendment
	4.	What events in Voltaire's life led him to be a proponent of free speech?
		a. He was exiled from France for mocking the government.
		b. He was angry about taxation without representation.
		c. He felt that monarchs repressed natural rights.
		d. He felt that Great Britain violated his social contract.
Score 3.0	5.	Describe how the developments of the Scientific Revolution contributed to the philosophical developments of the Enlightenment.
	6.	Explain how the U.S. Constitution is a social contract. Provide a specific example within your explanation.
Score 4.0	7.	Pick one of the following and develop an argument for why it is most important to the United States: natural rights, separation of powers, or freedom of speech.

Figure 4.2: Sample assessment aligned to proficiency scale levels, grade 8 civics.

When creating or revising assessments, classroom teachers can use the following steps to increase validity by aligning items to learning targets.

1. After learning about validity, immediately review your classroom assessment. Begin by referencing your proficiency scale or success criteria for the priority standard that the assessment intends to measure.

2. Look at each item to ensure it is, in fact, linked to the priority standard. Does it address one or more learning targets represented on the proficiency scale or within the success criteria?

3. Remove or revise any items you deem unrelated to the standard.

These steps ensure alignment to the learning targets. The process continues with checking for sufficiency of items.

Ensuring Sufficiency of Items

Once teachers feel confident their assessment items align with their learning targets, it is time to consider how many items students need to demonstrate mastery of the content or skill at each level of the scale. How many items are sufficient depends on several factors. One is the distribution of items across the scale levels. Teachers beginning their journey in standards-based learning might find that most items on their existing assessments align with the level of proficiency (score 3.0 on the proficiency scale). This certainly gives some information about a student's mastery or lack thereof; however, including all levels (basic, target, and advanced) allows teachers to ascertain the *degree* of proficiency students have attained. As mentioned previously (page 22), assessments early in the instructional cycle (preassessments and checks for understanding) might involve one or two levels, as students aren't yet expected to have mastered all the knowledge and skills. When considering the end-of-cycle assessment, we recommend a complete range of items.

Another factor is the stakes of the assessment. If there are lower stakes because there will be multiple assessments providing information about student learning, then perhaps three items each for score 2.0 and score 3.0 and one item for score 4.0 (seven total) might be adequate. However, if an assessment has higher stakes—this one assessment will be used to make bigger decisions about individual students such as graduation, retention, or special programming—then more items are needed. For instance, a higher-stakes assessment for a single scale might have six or eight items each for score 2.0 and score 3.0 and one or two items for score 4.0 (thirteen to eighteen total).

It is also imperative to consider the amount of information obtained from different types of assessment items. Constructed-response items provide more information than selected-response items. A few constructed-response items may yield the same amount of information (or more) about a student's understanding than a larger number of selected-response items.

Finally, teachers should consider the relationships between items. *Independent* items mean that a student does not have to get one item right to get another item correct. Closely related items are known as *dependent*. For example, if an assessment first asks students to graph the x and y intercepts and then asks questions about the resulting graph, students' answers to the second part depend on their drawing a correct graph as prompted in the first part (Heflebower, 2009).

The following steps continue the validity check begun in the previous section (page 71).

4. Does the assessment have questions that represent each of the proficiency scale levels?

5. How many items match each level?

6. What types of items (selected response, constructed response, and so on) match each level?

Ensuring Fair Classroom Assessments

Another essential component for reviewing the technical quality of classroom assessments is fairness. Authors Jay McTighe and Steven Ferrara (1998) explained this well when writing, "Fairness in classroom assessment refers to giving all students an equal chance to show what they know and can do" (p. 8; see also Gobble, Onuscheck, Reibel, & Twadell, 2016; Heflebower, Hoegh, & Warrick, 2017; Tankersley, 2007). Within fairness, there are three considerations.

1. Students have the opportunity to learn the content before the assessment.

2. Assessments are at the appropriate level—readability and expectations are congruent to the level of the learner.

3. Assessments are free from bias and will not unintentionally inhibit the performance of certain students or specific subgroups.

We discuss each factor in the following sections.

Opportunity to Learn

Providing students the opportunity to learn the content prior to the assessment is essential. Although this seems somewhat obvious, it does not always happen. For instance, imagine a middle school English teacher conducting a lesson on analyzing various pieces of literature. The teacher delves into an engaging comparative analysis and provides students with many examples throughout this lesson. In the teacher's mind, he may think he taught students to analyze literature. Yet the students did not learn to conduct such an analysis independently. When the students arrive for the classroom assessment on analyzing literature, they have never had the opportunity to perform this skill. This assessment is unintentionally unfair in that sense. The teacher facilitated a wonderful lesson, but students did not conduct their own analysis or receive feedback prior to being assessed.

If students have not had the opportunity to learn, the test will measure other factors that students bring to the classroom, like their background experiences, socioeconomic status, and English fluency. Teachers should review their classroom or team practices to ensure students have the opportunity to learn the priority standards before assessments. When reviewing or developing an assessment, double-check the content against your lesson and instructional cycle plans. Ask yourself, "Is the content of the assessment reflective of my lesson and unit plans? Did I actually teach this information and to what degree?" Using instructional-cycle plans with assessments included throughout, along with assessment blueprints, helps ensure that there won't be items on an assessment that weren't thoroughly taught during instruction.

Appropriate Assessment Levels

Assessments aligned to proficiency scales, as we have seen throughout this book, should ensure that the content of the assessment matches students' learning levels. Here we consider the appropriateness of other test features—reading passages, directions, and so on. We first approach this aspect of fairness from the perspective of readability. In other words, does the readability of the test match the students' reading level? It would be unfair for, say, a third-grade teacher to inadvertently use a reading passage that is at a fifth-grade readability level on an assessment. Or, consider a mathematics assessment for the same third-grade class. It would be unfair (and unnecessary) to write the directions in a complex way that includes challenging vocabulary.

There are various means for addressing appropriate readability. One way is to simply have grade-level teachers review the assessments. They would ask themselves, "Is this appropriate for a third-grade student?" or "Would the typical third-grade student be able to read this independently?" Another strategy is to conduct readability analyses using one of the many available software solutions. For example, Microsoft Word can assign a readability score to a document using the Flesch–Kincaid grade levels. Other readability analyses include, but are not limited to, Dale-Chall, Spache, and Lexile levels. Note, however, that readability programs have inherent measurement error. If the margin of error is, for example, one grade level, a passage scored as 8.0 (eighth grade) might be as low as seventh grade or as high as ninth grade. Readability analyses are not perfect, but they do provide a point of reference. Realistically, it is impossible to address readability perfectly for all students. What is readable for one may not be for another. The best course of action for a teacher or team of teachers is to ensure that the requirements of the standards are met *and* to consider whether they have done everything possible to minimize this particular type of fairness concern.

Another consideration of appropriate level is clarity. Directions, selected-response options, and other test features must be clear if the assessment is to provide accurate information about students. Items that are poorly written may prevent students from answering correctly, even if they know the content. One approach is simply to ask, "Is what the teacher asking clear?" Teachers should take their own tests with this question in mind before giving them to students. If you find yourself rereading a question or a sentence, likely it is not clearly written. It is always best to operate in a proactive manner and address potential problems before asking students to engage in the classroom assessment. This helps minimize confusion and frustration from students.

Bias Mitigation

One final consideration is to review assessments for bias. Bias simply means that some students may perform better or worse simply because of who they are and how the assessment items connect or do not connect with them. The following elements of bias should be avoided (Brookhart, 2012; Malouff, Stein, Bothma, Coulter, & Emmerton, 2014; Marzano et al., 2022; NDE, 2003, 2007).

- **Offensive content:** Strive to eliminate content that some students might perceive as offensive. Examples might include positive depictions of problematic activities like gambling or unnecessary references to sensitive historical events such as the Holocaust. This content may cause a student's emotions to impact their thinking or cause undue concern.

- **Stereotyping:** Test questions, reading passages, and other assessments sometimes play into cultural stereotypes. Avoid such depictions as a

Vietnamese American person pictured as a nail technician, a Mexican American person depicted eating tacos, and so on.

- **Unfair representation:** Be on the lookout for material where representation of different groups is unequal. Examples include using all masculine or all feminine names, depicting men in professional occupations while showing women and transgender or nonbinary people as service-industry workers, and depicting Asian Americans only as mathematics or science specialists.

- **Unfamiliar situations:** Avoid requiring background knowledge about situations that may be unfamiliar to certain subgroups. For example, a writing prompt that asks students to describe the state in which students reside would be unfairly challenging to students who recently moved from a different state or country. As another example, primary students might complete an activity matching the names of objects to pictures of those objects, which would be more difficult if a student has never seen some of the objects.

Ensuring Reliable Classroom Assessments

Addressing the concept of reliability is another important factor for quality: "Reliability is the degree to which students' results remain consistent over time or over replications of an assessment procedure" (Nitko & Brookhart, 2011, p. 23). In short, reliability involves consistency, accuracy, stability, and dependability in scoring. Just like you would want your kitchen scale to have these characteristics to ensure you are measuring ingredients accurately, classroom assessments need to be reliable to accurately guide student learning. What if your scale gave a different reading each time you weighed the same steak or bowl of flour? That scale would be unreliable, and you would not want to make cooking decisions based on its measurements. Student scores should remain consistent from one assessment to another about the very same topic if no instruction occurs during the interim. Obviously, teachers *do* want to see student scores improve *as their knowledge and skills improve.* Considering reliability ensures changing scores reflect changes in learning as opposed to poor assessment design.

Reliability ranges from 0 (or 0 percent) to 1.0 (or 100 percent). Zero indicates that the assessment has no reliability, and 1.0 means a perfect reliability. Because all assessments inherently have some measurement error, one should not expect to find 100 percent reliability. For standardized tests, a reliability of 0.80 (80 percent) or higher is very good (NDE, 2007). In fact, professor of measurement and statistics David A. Frisbie (1988) shared that most published assessments have reliabilities at or near 0.90 (90 percent). For example, the 2015 National Assessment of Educational Progress (NAEP) fourth-grade mathematics exam had a reliability of 90–100 percent for the constructed-response items (percentage of exact agreement; NAEP, 2021). Teacher-created assessments often come in much lower, at or near 0.50 (50 percent; Marzano, 2018). Teachers should strive for a reliability of 0.70 (70 percent) or higher for a classroom assessment (Feldt & Brennan, 1993; Marzano, 2018; NDE, 2007). Below that threshold, teachers should review the assessment and consider ways to increase the reliability. Some common ways to do this include the following.

- Lengthen the test. The more items, the more consistency or reliability.

- Manage item difficulty. Reconsider the review of how difficult items are and add, delete, or modify accordingly.

- Allow more time for students to complete the assessment.

- Manage item validity. Ensure that items actually measure the topic or content well.

- Replace items that display inconsistent or incongruent student-response patterns.

There are different ways to measure the reliability of classroom assessments. First, the teacher must match the type of assessment items with the appropriate method of reliability. *Objectively scored assessments* are those with selected-response items where there is a correct answer from which to select. *Subjectively scored assessments* are those with open-ended responses like short constructed-response items, extended constructed-response items, projects, and performances for which there may be multiple correct responses or variations of acceptable responses. The following sections describe reliability methods for each type of assessment.

Reliability Methods for Objectively Scored Assessments

In the following sections, we address four options for determining the reliability of objectively scored assessment types: (1) split-half, (2) test-retest, (3) parallel forms, and (4) decision consistency. When applying any of these four methods, it is best to use assessment data from thirty or more students.

Split-Half

Split-half is a reliability method used for selected-response items. In short, it involves splitting the assessment in half and determining whether students perform equally well on both halves. For example, one half is the even-numbered items and the second half is the odd-numbered assessment items. Each pair of items (items 1 and 2, items 3 and 4, and so on) is at the same level and about the same element of content. A twenty-item assessment would have ten pairs. After students take the assessment, the teacher can calculate the correlation between the first-half scores and the second-half scores. For instance, if a student gets item 1 correct, he should also get item 2 correct because they are about the same content and at the same level of complexity. If he misses item 3, he should also miss item 4. For each pair of items that match (both correct or both incorrect), the teacher would code it as 1. For each set of items that do not match, the teacher codes it as a 0 (Glen, 2022b; Heflebower, 2009; NDE, 2007).

Taking the ratio of matches to total pairs and converting it to a percentage provides a reliability score. For example, eight out of ten (8/10) matches would be 80 percent reliability. However, the teacher must calculate this ratio in aggregate for all students to get an accurate measure of the assessment's reliability. For instance, if three students had 7/10 matches, one student had 8/10, and one had 9/10, the number of matches would be 7 + 7 + 7 + 8 + 9 = 38. That number, divided by the total number of available pairs for five students (10 × 5 = 50), would therefore be 38/50 or 76 percent reliability. That would be considered a strong reliability for a classroom assessment. (However, note that teachers should use this process with at least thirty student scores.)

Test-Retest

This reliability method for objective assessments allows a teacher to measure the correlation (relationship) between two test administrations of the same assessment over time. This means giving the same test twice to the same students at different times, with no intervening instruction. Teachers are looking to see if students score very closely, if not identically, on each administration. For instance, a student that scores 18/20 on the first test administration should score around 18/20 for the second assessment administration. You would also anticipate that any items students miss on the first administration would be missed on the second, and any items answered correctly on the first are mastered on the second administration as well (Glen, 2022c; Heflebower, 2009; NDE, 2007). The overall reliability of the assessment is determined by comparing the number of students who performed similarly to the number of those who did not. For example, say that out of thirty students, twenty-two performed similarly between the two assessment administrations and eight did not. One would calculate the test-retest reliability by dividing 22/30, which equals about 0.73. As stated earlier, this is an acceptable reliability ratio.

With this method, teachers can also consider the correlation for individual items by looking at which items students answered consistently or inconsistently. For instance, you might notice student A missed items 3, 5, 6, and 7 on the first administration, and also missed those same items on the second administration. That means that the student's performance is consistent on the content of those items, as that student missed the same items on each administration.

This method is not very popular with teachers or students because of the time commitment: it requires a group of students to take the same test twice in a relatively short period of time and the teacher to score the same assessment twice. Nevertheless, test-retest is an acceptable method in the measurement literature and an option for classroom teachers.

Parallel Forms

This objective assessment reliability method allows a teacher to measure the correlation between two equivalent versions of one assessment. Some teachers already use a version of this strategy in their classrooms—especially in secondary schools. Teachers often create form A, form B, and maybe even form C versions of assessments, sometimes to mitigate cheating and other times to offer reassessment opportunities for students. The most common way teachers create parallel assessment forms is to first produce a large set of questions they would use to assess the same knowledge or skill. The questions are then randomly divided into two sets (or three if a form C is desired). Teachers can also use these different versions to determine internal consistency (reliability) of the assessment.

When using parallel assessment forms to compute assessment reliability, there are a few key considerations to note. First, the different versions need to have the same number of assessment items, directions, expectations, construct, and the like. Second, the forms need to employ similar item types. If form A has five selected-response items and three constructed-response items, then forms B and C should have the same distribution. Finally, the items on various forms should cover the same content. For example, item 1 on form A should address the same topic and level of content as item 1 on forms B and C, item 2 on each of the versions should relate to the same content, and so on (Glen, 2022a; Heflebower, 2009; NDE, 2007).

Ideally, the same students take all versions of the assessment, with each student scoring very similarly if not identically on each version. In this way, this method is similar to test-retest, except that students take different versions of the test instead of retaking the exact same set of questions. If using two forms of a test, divide students randomly into two groups. The first group completes form A while the second group completes form B, and then they switch. The number of students who scored the same on both forms is the raw score—if twenty-four out of thirty students had the same score on form A as on form B, the raw score is 24/30. That would constitute an 80 percent reliability, which is desirable.

However, it goes without saying that having one group of students take two sets of assessment items may be difficult or impractical and comes with the same downsides as the test-retest method. Therefore, teachers can modify this process slightly by comparing two groups of students. For example, perhaps a teacher has two sections of the same course: period 1 and period 2. They learn the same content from the same teacher, so they are comparable. Did proficient students (based on evidence noted on assignments and class discussions) taking form A in period 1 mirror performance from proficient students taking form B in period 2? In order to determine the degree of reliability through parallel forms, the teacher compares the performances of the two groups of students. For example, say twenty out of thirty students (66 percent) in period 1 score proficient on the assessment as compared to twenty-two out of twenty-eight students (78 percent) in period 2. These percentages are quite different, suggesting a lack of reliability.

Another way to check internal consistency is to make some items identical on both forms. For instance, perhaps items 3, 5, 7, 9, 11, 13, and 15 are the exact same on form A and form B. The teacher would then compare how similar students taking different versions of the test performed on those matched items. Did the proficient students from period 1 taking form A score the same on the identical items as proficient students from period 2 taking form B? Although such modifications may not constitute a pure method, they still help the teacher or team see how assessments items function, thus providing insights into the assessment's internal consistency.

Decision Consistency

Another method for figuring reliability for objective assessment types is known as *decision consistency*. This method can also be used with subjectively scored assessments (NDE, 2007; Thompson, 2018).

This method is helpful since teachers can use it with any number of students. It requires two independent decisions about students' performances on the assessment. The two decisions could consist of either (1) assessment results from two different assessments that measure the same content at the same level of difficulty, or (2) a teacher's judgment and the results of an assessment. In short, this method involves calculating the percentage of times the two decisions agree.

Comparing a teacher's judgment and the results of an assessment is typically the more practical method for classroom teachers. The steps of this process are as follows (NDE, 2007).

1. The teachers review the proficiency scales to ensure they have consistent expectations for student performance at each of the levels.

2. Teachers make predictions as to the performance level they believe each of their students will achieve and record their judgments as a score. This personal judgment based on classroom interactions needs to be made *before* the teachers actually know the results from the assessment.

3. The teachers score the assessment and record students' scores.

4. Teachers compare their judgments and students' actual scores. If the teacher judgment and the actual results are identical, the teachers record an indication of agreement such as a +; if not, they record the disagreement as a *0* or similar.

5. The ratio of agreements to total number of decisions is then converted into a percentage. If there are sixteen agreements out of twenty students, that percentage of decision consistency would be 80 percent. This is an acceptable reliability.

Reliability Methods for Subjectively Scored Assessments

There are also different options for figuring the reliability of subjective assessment types. We describe these in the following sections.

Inter-Rater Reliability

Inter-rater reliability compares how two different teachers score the same student performances or artifacts. It should not matter which teacher scores a student's assessment—the score should be an accurate and consistent reflection of the student's performance. This method is well known among educators and fairly easy to employ. It is especially useful for collaborative teams who need to ensure that members are scoring their common assessments in a consistent manner. The steps of determining inter-rater reliability are as follows (Heflebower et al., 2021; NDE, 2007).

1. Teachers review the scoring rubric or criteria for the subjectively scored assessment. Knowing the assessment purposes and how the assessment will be used is helpful in their scoring. They also examine exemplars (such as student products or anchor papers) showcasing all proficiency levels. This provides a picture of how the various results may look.

2.   Raters (that is, the teachers) score each student's assessment individually and record their independent scores.

3.   Teachers compare their scores for each student's assessment and record whether they agreed or disagreed (perhaps using + and *0*)

4.   The reliability percentage is figured by dividing the number of agreements by the total number of students and converting to a percentage. For instance, if teachers agreed on seven out of nine students' scores, that would equate to 77 percent reliability.

Intra-Rater Reliability

While inter-rater reliability considers the consistency between teachers, *intra-rater reliability* concerns whether an individual teacher scores various students' work consistently. Most educators assume they are quite dependable as they score a group of student assessments, but human judgment is influenced by factors like time of day, fatigue level, distraction level, opinions about students, and so on. A few simple strategies can heighten awareness and increase reliability quite considerably (Heflebower et al., 2021; Gareis & Grant, 2015).

- Cover students' names while scoring or have students write their names on the back of their work. Knowing which student an assessment belongs to may inadvertently increase or decrease the teacher's opinions of the correctness of the responses. Feelings about and perceptions of students may unintentionally affect how teachers score them.

- Score one constructed-response item all the way through the set of assessments. This way, the expected criteria for that item are fresh and top of mind. For instance, if item 4 is a short-answer item, assess item 4 on all students' tests before scoring item 5 on any student's assessment. When teachers score each student's entire test in turn, they have to change focus continuously, which may affect objectivity and thus reliability.

- Review the criteria for a constructed-response item each time you evaluate a new item. Look back at the scoring guide, rubric, or proficiency scale to ensure the criteria are top of mind prior to scoring each student's response.

- Shuffle the assessments between scoring each constructed-response item or section of an assessment (or randomize them, if in an online format). This way, students are not always scored at the beginning, middle, or end of the scoring round or session. Fatigue and distraction can set in as teachers progress through scoring a given item, affecting reliability.

These methods for ensuring assessment reliability may seem complex or unusual, but the most important idea for any teacher to remember is that scoring must be consistent across all students. By making sure scoring practices are consistent, you can make accurate decisions about student performance.

Ensuring Appropriate Mastery Levels

Assessments designed based on proficiency scales lend themselves to scoring based on scales as well. (See chapter 5, page 87, for a complete discussion of standards-based scoring practices.) However, some teachers might want to score assessments using a traditional points-based or percentage system. But that raises the question, What percentage indicates that a student is proficient? To answer that, we discuss setting proficiency cut scores on classroom assessments.

A *proficiency cut score* is that fine line that separates students who demonstrate the knowledge and skills deemed necessary for mastery of a priority standard or learning target and those who do not yet demonstrate such knowledge and skills (Heflebower, 2009). By using a robust process to set cut scores for assessments, teachers can avoid making arbitrary scoring decisions. Cut scores also account for assessments of varying difficulty. Imagine two students who have the same level of understanding on a particular topic. One takes an easy test and scores very well; the other takes a more difficult test and scores much lower. The different cut scores for the two assessments will show that both are proficient.

There are four methods for setting classroom assessment cut scores that individual classroom teachers or a team of teachers can implement.

Modified Contrasting Group Method

The modified contrasting group method is a student-centered method that requires teachers know their students and those students' typical performances. It is used with empirical evidence obtained from how students score on the assessment (NDE, 2007).

1. The teacher reviews the proficiency scales and becomes familiar with them and what each level of the scale means.

2. Prior to actually scoring the assessment, the teacher makes a prediction, based on professional judgment, about how each student will perform (beginning, progressing, proficient, or advanced). The teacher records these predictions on a chart by marking an X in the appropriate column (see figure 4.3, page 82).

3. After scoring the assessment, the teacher replaces the X for each student with the student's actual percentage score (see figure 4.4, page 82).

4. The teacher averages the student scores in each column (beginning, progressing, proficient, or advanced), as exemplified in figure 4.4 (page 82).

5. Finally, the teacher sets cut scores between each level by taking the average of adjacent column averages, as seen in figure 4.4. For instance, the mean of the beginning column average and the progressing column average becomes the cut score between beginning and progressing.

The cut scores provide guidance as to how to determine the level of performance for each student. When students' percentage scores are below the lowest cut score—65 percent in the example—they are in the beginning range (score 1.0). In the example, if they score between 65 and 83 percent, that is the classification of score 2.0. If they score between 84 and 93 percent, that is classified as proficient (score 3.0), and 94 percent and above is advanced.

Student Name	Beginning (1.0)	Progressing (2.0)	Proficient (3.0)	Advanced (4.0)
Juan			X	
Sarah	X			
Julio		X		
Ken				X
Josie			X	
Cully		X		
Denise			X	
Michaela				X

Figure 4.3: Initial student performance predictions (modified contrasting group method).

Student Name	Beginning (1.0)	Progressing (2.0)	Proficient (3.0)	Advanced (4.0)
Juan			92 percent	
Sarah	52 percent			
Julio		71 percent		
Ken				99 percent
Josie			89 percent	
Cully		84 percent		
Denise			91 percent	
Michaela				95 percent
Average Column Score Percent	52 percent	77.5 percent	91 percent	97 percent

Cut Score Percent

▲ 65 percent   ▲ 84 percent   ▲ 94 percent

Figure 4.4: Modified contrasting group method cut scores.

Visit MarzanoResources.com/reproducibles for a blank reproducible version of this figure.

Bookmark Method

One method that is often used in larger-scale assessments is called the *bookmark method*. In this method, item difficulty is determined prior to assessment administration based on proficiency scales, and teachers review a document where the items are presented in order of difficulty (easiest to hardest). Each teacher looks through the entire set once to read every item. Then, they go back through the items and, based on professional judgment, place a "bookmark" at the point in the item set that represents the cut point between proficient and not proficient. They would then add bookmarks for any additional cut points. If there were four classifications, such as (1) beginning, (2) progressing, (3) proficient, and (4) advanced, then teachers would place three bookmarks (Karantonis

& Sireci, 2006). Teachers can compare bookmarks with their collaborative team members and come to collective decisions about the cut points for common assessments.

Modified Analytical Judgment

Another method for figuring cut scores that classroom teachers can use is the modified analytical-judgment method (Cizek, 2012; NDE, 2007). Teachers can use this method with any number of students and on either objectively scored assessments or those more subjective in nature, like constructed-response items. Since it includes the use of exemplars, it is actually a better fit for subjective assessments.

1. Examine the proficiency scale and look at the content of each level.

2. Discuss the characteristics of student work at the progressing, proficient, and advanced levels.

3. Select exemplars of the assessment for each level. Teachers should not know the scores when selecting them.

4. Average the actual scores of the exemplars selected for each cut score.

5. Determine the ranges by calculating them from the cut scores. For example, progressing might be 71–80 percent, proficient might be 81–90 percent, and advanced 91–100 percent.

Modified Angoff Method

The final method for determining cut scores we will discuss is the modified Angoff method (Cizek, 2012; Impara & Plake, 1998; NDE, 2007). It, too, can be used with any number of students and on either objectively or subjectively scored assessments. Teachers using this method must know both the assessment content and the characteristics of the students taking the assessment. The teacher analyzes each item on the assessment in relationship to student performance. The following steps outline the process, and figure 4.5 (page 84) exemplifies the process.

1. Call to mind a student who barely reaches each proficiency level (beginning, progressing, proficient, and advanced)—that is, a student who just reaches the minimum requirements of the level.

2. Look at the first item on the assessment. Would you expect the barely advanced student to answer this question correctly? If so, put a 1 on the chart under Advanced. If not, record a 0.

3. Then consider the barely proficient student. If you would expect them to answer item 1 correctly, put a 1 on the chart under Proficient. If not, record a 0.

4. Then consider the barely progressing student. If you would expect them to answer item 1 correctly, put a 1 on the chart under Progressing. If not, record a 0.

5. Then consider the beginning student. If you would expect them to answer item 1 correctly, put a 1 on the chart under Beginning. If not, record a 0.

6. Continue this method for each item on the assessment, considering one item at a time and working from barely advanced down for each one. When you reach the level at which you determine the student would *not* get the item correct, write a 0 on the chart for that level and each lower level.

7. Add up the number of 1s for each performance level. Record the total at the bottom of each column.

8. Use the totals to determine the minimum cut score for each level of proficiency and set mastery ranges. The ranges for progressing, proficient, and advanced should begin with the total and end with one less than the total in the next-higher column.

9. Record the range for each proficiency level in the chart. After scoring students' assessments, compare students' scores to the ranges to determine whether they are beginning, progressing, proficient, or advanced on the topic.

Assessment Item Number	Beginning (1.0)	Progressing (2.0)	Proficient (3.0)	Advanced (4.0)
1	0	1	1	1
2	0	0	1	1
3	0	0	0	1
4	0	0	0	0
5	1	1	1	1
6	0	0	1	1
7	0	0	1	1
8	0	0	0	1
9	1	1	1	1
10	0	0	0	1
Totals	2	3	6	9
Ranges	0–2 items correct	3–5 items correct	6–8 items correct	9–10 items correct

Figure 4.5: Modified Angoff method chart.

Note that this example assumes each item is either correct or incorrect. For assessments where students can be partially correct on certain items or where items are worth multiple points, teachers can easily adjust this strategy. Instead of marking 1 or 0, record the number of points you expect the barely progressing, barely proficient, and barely advanced students to earn on each item (NDE, 2007). On a four-point item, for example, perhaps the teacher decides that a barely advanced student would earn four points, a barely proficient student would also earn all four points, and a barely progressing student would earn two points. Total the columns and assign ranges using the same approach. The ranges will be in terms of points earned rather than items correct.

Summary

Reviewing assessments for technical quality is important in a standards-based learning environment. In this chapter, we detailed the technical characteristics for individual teacher and teacher team consideration. Begin with your own classroom and take small steps to improve assessments by applying the criterion of validity to be certain the assessment measures what you intend. Next, apply the considerations of fairness so that students aren't inadvertently penalized due to conditions beyond their control. Then, use practical processes to ensure your classroom assessments and scoring procedures function reliably and reflect students' knowledge rather than chance errors. Finally, consider using mastery cut scores to help determine the difficulty of your assessment items when figuring scores for students. Bestselling author Malcolm Gladwell (2000) noted poor practice "can be reversed, can be tipped, by tinkering with the smallest of details of the immediate environment" (p. 142). Review a classroom assessment you use and find a place you feel comfortable starting to revise your practice, and then do it. As you enact technical quality within your classroom, students will benefit.

Chapter 4 Reflection Questions

1. What is important for a classroom teacher to know about validity?

2. What are three important considerations regarding fairness that a classroom teacher needs to apply to assessments?

3. What are some different methods for determining whether an assessment functions in a reliable manner?

4. How might a teacher or team of teachers determine proficiency cut scores for an assessment?

5. Thinking of a unit you have taught or currently teach, how might you apply the concepts or strategies discussed in this chapter?

5

The Process of Scoring Assessments

Key idea: It is important that classroom teachers give significant thought to the scoring of assessments. This helps ensure that accurate information is available for decision-making processes based on assessment results.

Once the assessment administration process is complete, it is time for a classroom teacher or team of teachers to score the assessment. The end goal of the scoring process is accurate information that represents the level of learning for individual students and the entire group of students as a whole. As mentioned in chapter 3 (page 51), we recommend determining scoring guidance prior to giving assessments, especially end-of-cycle assessments. Considering scoring guidance in advance minimizes the potential for poor-quality assessment items, as teachers have scoring in mind as they examine each item. With this preparation in mind, there are multiple considerations for teachers as they approach the scoring process. This chapter provides information about scoring different item types and determining final scores.

Scoring Different Item Types

Classroom assessments that are based on proficiency scales consist of different item types, which we discuss in chapter 2 (page 19). Here, we provide an overview of how to score those various item types.

Selected-Response Items

Selected-response items are the easiest item type to score because of their right-or-wrong nature. In other words, students respond either correctly or incorrectly to this type of item. The simplest way to score these items is to mark each response *correct* (often abbreviated to *C*) or *incorrect* (abbreviated to *I*). Using this response-coding method, a teacher would score each individual item and then consider how many questions the student answered correctly to help determine the overall proficiency scale score for the assessment (see page 93). Some teachers like to assign points to assessment items as a method for assigning the overall score. When this is the case, each selected-response item should be worth one point—the teacher scores each selected-response item as *1* or *0*. Because selected-response items cannot be partially correct, it is unnecessary and potentially confusing to assign, say, five points to each selected-response item.

Constructed-Response Items

The scoring of constructed-response items, whether they are short-answer or extended response, takes a little more thought and preparation than selected-response items. These item types are open ended, often with numerous possible correct responses. As mentioned previously, we encourage teachers and teams to discuss scoring prior to giving the assessment, especially when it is an end-of-cycle assessment. The practice of setting scoring criteria and sharing that guidance or rubric with students helps ensure that students have all the information they need to craft acceptable and appropriate responses. It also helps streamline the scoring process for teachers, because the scoring guidance already exists and now teachers can simply apply it.

Short constructed-response items require students to write or say a short phrase, write or say a few sentences, or draw symbols or simple depictions. Sometimes, a short constructed-response item is either correct or incorrect. For example, the prompt "Write one detail about the setting of the story" would have clear correct and incorrect answers. When this is the case, scoring is very similar to selected response in that the teacher can mark the answer *C* or *I* or assign one point.

More frequently, however, a constructed-response item is open ended and the response has degrees of completeness or correctness. Again, it is important that teachers discuss these possibilities prior to scoring and set criteria or use previous student work or teacher-generated exemplars (as described in chapter 3, page 51). The following constructed-response item is one that could have quite a few acceptable student responses.

> What might have happened at the end of the story if the main character had chosen to do things differently?

While it is a short-answer item, students may make very different predictions. Thinking about possible answers or determining what features of a response indicate student knowledge is very helpful in ensuring efficient scoring.

Constructed response also includes extended-response items that require students to write longer compositions in response to multipart prompts. This item type frequently appears on end-of-cycle assessments, especially in relation to scores 3.0 and 4.0 on the proficiency scale. The scoring process is similar to our recommendations for short-answer items, including teacher-generated possible responses and student papers as anchors. However, scoring guides or rubrics are more common and more detailed with extended-response items. An example of a secondary mathematics scoring guide appears in figure 5.1. These criteria give teachers guidance to score subjective answers consistently. To minimize subjectivity even further, this scoring guide could be used in tandem with anchors—authentic student products that serve as examples of different scores.

Criteria	Ratings			Points Earned and Feedback
Mathematization and Modeling Does the response mathematize the situation accurately?	2 points Correct: The response describes mathematics that make sense for this question.	1 point Partially correct: The response partially describes mathematics that make sense for this question but some elements are missing.	0 points Incorrect: The mathematics don't make sense or response doesn't represent a good attempt. The student might have written "IDK" or "My brain told me."	
Connect to Context Does the response connect to the context?	2 points Correct: The response connects to the context completely. I don't have any questions about what the student is describing or explaining.	1 point Partially correct: The response is tenuously connected to the context. I have some questions about what the student is describing or explaining.	0 points Incorrect: The response is not connected to the context or doesn't represent a good attempt. The student might have written "IDK" or "My brain told me."	
Logic Is the response logical?	2 points Correct: The response is logical. I can follow the student's thinking throughout the response.	1 point Partially correct: The response is sometimes logical. There are times I am not able to follow the student's thinking.	0 points Incorrect: The response is illogical or doesn't represent a good attempt. The student might have written "IDK" or "My brain told me."	

Source: © 2021 by San Diego Unified School District. Adapted with permission.

Figure 5.1: Sample scoring guide, secondary mathematics.

One other feature to note about the scoring guide is that it has three possible levels of performance for each criterion, therefore creating quite a few possible outcomes, as shown in figure 5.2 (page 90). The right column shows the overall score, based on the level of accuracy in the student's response for each criterion. Notice that all three criteria must be assigned two points to earn full credit.

Score for Mathematization and Modeling	Score for Connect to Context	Score for Logic	Overall Score for This Extended-Response Item
2 points	2 points	2 points	6 points (full credit)
1 point	2 points	2 points	5 points (high partial credit)
2 points	1 point	2 points	5 points (high partial credit)
2 points	2 points	1 point	5 points (high partial credit)
2 points	1 point	1 point	4 points (low partial credit)
1 point	1 point	2 points	4 points (low partial credit)
1 point	2 points	1 point	4 points (low partial credit)
1 point	1 point	1 point	3 points (no credit)
0 points	1 point	1 point	2 points (no credit)
1 point	0 points	0 point	1 point (no credit)

Figure 5.2: Possible scoring outcomes, secondary mathematics.

There are also times when a teacher or team chooses to use response codes, such as *C* (correct), *PC* (partially correct), and *I* (incorrect), for extended-response items. For example, consider the following item on an end-of-cycle assessment for third-grade ELA.

> Determine a character trait for the main character in the story. Decide whether the trait had a positive or negative impact on another character or the overall outcome of the story. Be sure to provide evidence from the story to support your decision.

In this case, to receive full credit a student must meet all three requirements: character trait for main character, positive or negative impact, and evidence to support the decision. The teacher could code each element of each student's response as correct or incorrect and determine an overall score based on how many of the three are correct. The key takeaway from this section is that teachers and teams must establish scoring guides for extended-response items prior to administering assessments.

Performance Assessments

Performance assessments are scored using the rubric created for use with the assessment. McTighe (2013) identified two kinds of rubrics—*holistic* and *analytic*:

> A holistic rubric provides an overall impression of a student's work. Holistic rubrics yield a single score or rating for a product or performance. An analytic rubric divides a product or performance into distinct traits or dimensions and judges each separately. Since an analytic rubric rates each of the identified traits independently, a separate score is provided for each. (p. 91)

Both types of rubrics can be used with performance assessments. The choice largely depends on the purpose of the assessment and the amount of feedback the teacher wishes to provide to the student. If the assessment is intended to rate overall student performance on a learning goal, then a holistic rubric may be sufficient.

Consider the sample holistic rubric in figure 5.3 for eighth-grade drama students performing a monologue. It is relatively simple, designed to give general feedback on some aspects of the learning targets engaged by the performance assessment. This rubric provides students a vision of the teacher's expectations, although it is still somewhat broad.

Drama Performance and Rehearsal	
4	• Monologue is substantially refined and improved beyond the level of a classroom performance. • Physical, vocal, and physiological aspects of the performance are refined through rehearsal beyond the level of a classroom performance.
3	• Monologue is effectively revised using repetition and analysis. • Physical, vocal, and physiological aspects of the performance are effectively refined through rehearsal.
2	• Monologue is partially revised using repetition and analysis. • Physical, vocal, and physiological aspects of the performance are partially refined through rehearsal.
1	• Monologue is ineffectively revised using repetition and analysis. • Physical, vocal, and physiological aspects of the performance are ineffectively refined through rehearsal.

Figure 5.3: Sample holistic rubric for performance rehearsal, grade 8 drama.

If teachers wish to give greater clarity on the expectations or assess students on multiple standards within the same assessment, an analytic rubric is appropriate. It facilitates more substantial and specific feedback to the student. Figure 5.4 (page 92) displays an analytic rubric for the same assessment as figure 5.3, highlighting the greater level of specificity. With an analytic rubric, students have the information they need to prepare in a specific way on many levels in creating the performance for this assessment.

Again, we should emphasize how the purpose of the assessment determines which type of rubric to use. A holistic rubric may well provide enough information for students to create a high-quality performance on an assessment, particularly if the assessment is low stakes or one of a series. In this case, analytic rubrics might be overkill—the student has far too much to monitor in preparing for the task. On the other hand, if the purpose of the assessment is to gauge student performance near the end of the instructional cycle, where many key factors will be evaluated in a single performance assessment, and where students have substantially more time to prepare the performance for the assessment, then an analytic rubric would be more appropriate.

When creating a rubric, whether holistic or analytic, teachers should be careful to restrict the number of criteria to an amount that gives clear guidance to the student about the requirements of the assessment but does not overwhelm the student. It is the nature of performance assessment that the teacher can evaluate an activity or product in multiple areas. Restricting the number of criteria to those specifically addressed in the instruction that precedes the assessment helps students see the relevance of the assessment and will help them feel they can handle the demands of the assessment.

Rubrics, of course, also guide teachers as they score performance assessments. Usually, teachers have a form that captures the rubric and provides space to record a score on each criterion. Two examples of such a form, aligned to the drama performance rubrics in figure 5.3 and figure 5.4 (page 92), respectively, appear in figure 5.5 (page 93) and figure 5.6 (page 94).

	Above Mastery	**Mastery of Grade-Level Standards**	**Approaching Mastery**	**Novice**
Scoring Criteria	4	3	2	1
Vocal Technique DTA09-GR.8-S.2	• Actor utilized adept vocal techniques with specific choices to find the voice of the character (intonation and connotation, subtext revealed, and vocal emotion).	• Actor clearly projected an articulate voice with vocal variety (pitch, rate, tone, tempo, volume, inflection) throughout the scene.	• Actor showed some difficulties in dialogue articulation and projection, resulting in difficulty of understanding; vocal variety techniques were lacking.	• Actor did not project or articulate; no vocal variety to express the character.
Movement and Stage Presence DTA09-GR.8-S.1–2	• Blocking, gestures, facial expressions, and posture created a new insight into the text and character. • Actor maintained a grounded presence, utilizing levels and positioning to create a believable character.	• Blocking, gestures, facial expressions, and posture were motivated by the text. • Actor represented a character that is grounded while demonstrating proper stage positioning.	• Blocking and gesturing appeared non-intuitive, causing a disconnect from the text. • Actor demonstrated a character that is not grounded (posture and presence that is indicative of the character) within the scene.	• Actor displayed no variety in movement or improvisational blocking of the scene. There were frequent break downs of traditional blocking rules, such as upstaging and not being open. • The character onstage represented the student and not the textual identify.
Characterization DTA09-GR.8-S.1–2	• Actor brought individuality to character. • Actor employed active tactics connected to character. • Actor took risks within framework of given circumstances.	• Actor sustained believability connected to the text. • All the actor's choices were well defined: obstacle, tactic, motivation, subtext, mannerisms, and physicality.	• Believable moments occurred within piece. • Character development was evident. • Actor exhibited two to three choices: obstacle, tactic, motivation, subtext, mannerisms, or physicality.	• Characterization was not believable or present. • Actor exhibited no or only one choice: obstacle, tactic, motivation, subtext, mannerisms, or physicality.
Relationship DTA09-GR.8-S.1–2	• Actor clearly defined relationships with others in the scene. Relationships were ever changing and reactionary within the scene.	• Actor demonstrated relationship through conflict (opposing objectives, creating obstacles, and tension).	• Actor appeared to be engaged in a monologue and not reacting to others within the scene.	• Actor actively chose to ignore the interactions needed to be within the moment.
Performance Fundamentals DTA09-GR.8-S.2	• Actor engaged others in a professional process through leadership.	• Actor memorized selection; professionalism, slate, and etiquette are evident.	• Actor hesitated within dialogue, slate was incorrect, and professionalism lacking.	• Actor did not memorize, did not slate, and showed poor theater etiquette, such as breaking focus, being distracted, lacking effort and understanding of the task, and missing entrances.
Self-Reflection DTA09-GR.8-S.3	• Actor's goals were determined by areas of weakness identified within the completed rubric.	• Actor's analysis and synthesis of performance contributed to the completed rubric and justified the score.	• Actor completed rubric without justification for selections.	• Actor only partially completed or did not fill out rubric.
Peer Critique DTA09-GR.8-S.3	• Actor provided constructive feedback relevant to this rubric, class goals, and objectives.	• Actor's analysis and synthesis of peers' performance contributed to the completed rubric and justified their score.	• Feedback was incomplete, lacking support and justifications.	• Performance viewed but no feedback provided.

Source: Adapted from Colorado Department of Education, n.d.b.

Figure 5.4: Sample analytic rubric for performance rehearsal, grade 8 drama.

Drama Performance Assessment		
Name: _____ Period: _____ Date: _____		

	Drama Performance and Rehearsal	Score	Comments
4	• Monologue is substantially refined and improved beyond the level of a classroom performance. • Physical, vocal, and physiological aspects of the performance are refined through rehearsal beyond the level of a classroom performance.		
3	• Monologue is effectively revised using repetition and analysis. • Physical, vocal, and physiological aspects of the performance are effectively refined through rehearsal.		
2	• Monologue is partially revised using repetition and analysis. • Physical, vocal, and physiological aspects of the performance are partially refined through rehearsal.		
1	• Monologue is ineffectively revised using repetition and analysis. • Physical, vocal, and physiological aspects of the performance are ineffectively refined through rehearsal.		

Figure 5.5: Sample scoring form with holistic rubric, grade 8 drama.

Before students perform, teachers should familiarize themselves with the details of the rubric. This makes it easier to focus on the specific criteria the rubric requires while scoring a performance. Simply using a blank form for each student, the teacher can indicate individual student performance on each criterion of the rubric and record written remarks as appropriate. This makes scoring efficient for the teacher, but also provides the possibility of providing detailed feedback to students.

Assigning Overall Assessment Scores

After scoring individual assessment items, the teacher must determine each student's overall score for the assessment. This overall score tells the teacher how each student is performing relative to the proficiency scale. The teacher then uses that information to plan next steps for instruction. This section discusses scoring assessments that cover a single learning target or a single level on a proficiency scale, assessments that include items from all three levels of a proficiency scale, and assessments that address multiple proficiency scales.

Drama Performance Assessment						
Name: _____ Period: _____ Date: _____						
	Above Mastery	**Mastery of Grade-Level Standards**	**Approaching Mastery**	**Novice**		
Scoring Criteria	4	3	2	1	Score	Comments
Vocal Technique DTA09-GR.8-S.2	• Actor utilized adept vocal techniques with specific choices to find the voice of the character (intonation and connotation, subtext revealed, and vocal emotion).	• Actor clearly projected an articulate voice with vocal variety (pitch, rate, tone, tempo, volume, inflection) throughout the scene.	• Actor showed some difficulties in dialogue articulation and projection, resulting in difficulty of understanding; vocal variety techniques were lacking.	• Actor did not project or articulate; no vocal variety to express the character.		
Movement and Stage Presence DTA09-GR.8-S.1–2	• Blocking, gestures, facial expressions, and posture created a new insight into the text and character. • Actor maintained a grounded presence, utilizing levels and positioning to create a believable character.	• Blocking, gestures, facial expressions, and posture were motivated by the text. • Actor represented a character that is grounded while demonstrating proper stage positioning.	• Blocking and gesturing appeared non-intuitive, causing a disconnect from the text. • Actor demonstrated a character that is not grounded (posture and presence that is indicative of the character) within the scene.	• Actor displayed no variety in movement or improvisational blocking of the scene. There were frequent break downs of traditional blocking rules, such as upstaging and not being open. • The character onstage represented the student and not the textual identify.		
Characterization DTA09-GR.8-S.1–2	• Actor brought individuality to character. • Actor employed active tactics connected to character. • Actor took risks within framework of given circumstances.	• Actor sustained believability connected to the text. • All the actor's choices were well defined: obstacle, tactic, motivation, subtext, mannerisms, and physicality.	• Believable moments occurred within piece. • Character development was evident. • Actor exhibited two to three choices: obstacle, tactic, motivation, subtext, mannerisms, or physicality.	• Characterization was not believable or present. • Actor exhibited no or only one choice: obstacle, tactic, motivation, subtext, mannerisms, or physicality.		

Relationship DTA09-GR.8-S.1–2	• Actor clearly defined relationships with others in the scene. Relationships were ever changing and reactionary within the scene.	• Actor demonstrated relationship through conflict (opposing objectives, creating obstacles, and tension).	• Actor appeared to be engaged in a monologue and not reacting to others within the scene.	• Actor actively chose to ignore the interactions needed to be within the moment.		
Performance Fundamentals DTA09-GR.8-S.2	• Actor engaged others in a professional process through leadership.	• Actor memorized selection; professionalism, slate, and etiquette are evident.	• Actor hesitated within dialogue, slate was incorrect, and professionalism lacking.	• Actor did not memorize, did not slate, and showed poor theater etiquette, such as breaking focus, being distracted, lacking effort and understanding of the task, and missing entrances.		
Self-Reflection DTA09-GR.8-S.3	• Actor's goals were determined by areas of weakness identified within the completed rubric.	• Actor's analysis and synthesis of performance contributed to the completed rubric and justified the score.	• Actor completed rubric without justification for selections.	• Actor only partially completed or did not fill out rubric.		
Peer Critique DTA09-GR.8-S.3	• Actor provided constructive feedback relevant to this rubric, class goals, and objectives.	• Actor's analysis and synthesis of peers' performance contributed to the completed rubric and justified their score.	• Feedback was incomplete, lacking support and justifications.	• Performance viewed, but no feedback provided.		

Source: Adapted from Colorado Department of Education, n.d.b.

Figure 5.6: Sample scoring form with analytic rubric, grade 8 drama.

Scoring Assessments for a Single Learning Target or a Single Level on a Proficiency Scale

As we discussed in chapter 2 (page 19), assessment will occur throughout the course of an instructional cycle. The teacher administers checks for understanding to ensure that students are absorbing the content as the opportunity to learn occurs. Checks for understanding and other brief or informal assessments may only address a single learning target or a single level on the proficiency scale. For example, teachers often instruct lessons on the score 2.0 content early in the instructional cycle and then check for understanding of that content to ensure students have mastered the basics before moving on to score

3.0 content. Suppose that a high school algebra I team is teaching a unit on solving quadratic equations. On day four of the fifteen-day unit, the teachers plan to offer a check for understanding on the score 2.0 content. Perhaps this assessment is a quiz consisting of four items related to the two score 2.0 learning targets, *I can simplify a square root* and *I can factor a quadratic expression*. The team of teachers has decided that students must answer all four items correctly in order to demonstrate mastery of the score 2.0 content. Their rationale is that they need that amount of evidence to feel confident that students have acquired the necessary foundational knowledge. Figure 5.7 shows possible scores that students can earn—the teachers have determined in advance possible score levels as well as the degree of correctness associated with each score level. Since the assessment only covers score 2.0 content, the highest possible score is 2.0.

Score 2.0	All four items correct
Score 1.5	Three items correct
Score 1.0	Two or fewer items correct

Figure 5.7: Possible scoring outcomes, algebra I check for understanding.

Scoring Assessments That Include All Three Levels of a Proficiency Scale

Some assessments include items that address all three levels of a proficiency scale (score 2.0 content, score 3.0 content, and score 4.0 content). This is most common for end-of-cycle assessments. These holistic assessments support teachers' decision making about students' current levels of performance on the proficiency scale. It also makes it more likely that all students experience some degree of success on the assessment. Consider the following fifth-grade mathematics proficiency scale (figure 5.8) and related end-of-cycle assessment (figure 5.9).

Score 4.0	Complex content: Convert a unit of measure from one measurement system to another.
Score 3.0	Target content: Convert like measurement units within a given measurement system (for example, centimeters to meters).
Score 2.0	Foundational content: Recognize that meters, grams, and liters are the base metric units for distance, weight, and mass. Recognize that feet, pounds, and gallons are the base U.S. units for distance, weight, and mass.

Source: © 2016 by Marzano Resources. Adapted with permission.

Figure 5.8: Proficiency scale for measurement conversions, grade 5 mathematics.

As you can see, this assessment includes items for all three levels on the proficiency scale. Prior to giving the end-of-cycle assessment, the team of fifth-grade teachers collaboratively determined the scoring guidance shown in figure 5.10 (page 98). Teachers simply score the assessments and apply the guidance to determine the final scores.

Name: _____   Date: _____

Score 2.0

1. Organize the words from the word bank into their correct measurement system and category. Some boxes will have more than one word and some words might not be used.

	Metric System	U.S. Customary Units
Distance		
Weight		
Mass		
Word Bank		
pound liter gram foot ton ounce meter scale inch yard gallon		

Score 3.0

2. Determine the answer to each question. Show your work and write your answer in the box.

   a. An adult elephant can weigh as much as seven tons. About how many pounds does an adult elephant weigh?

   b. Mario needs to cut pieces of ribbon that are each one meter long to tie onto balloons. If he has three pieces of ribbon that are each one decameter long, how many one-meter pieces of ribbon can he cut?

Score 4.0

3. Carly and Maria are working together on measuring pieces of yarn. Carly measured two pieces of yarn to be 4.5 inches long and 6.7 inches long. Maria measured two pieces of yarn to be 3.7 centimeters long and 6.4 centimeters long. What is the total length of all their yarn in customary units? Show your work and write your answer in the box.

Figure 5.9: Sample assessment covering all three levels, grade 5 mathematics.

Score 4.0	Student meets the score 3.0 requirements *and* responds correctly to the score 4.0 item.
Score 3.5	Student meets the score 3.0 requirements *and* responds partially correctly to the score 4.0 items.
Score 3.0	Student meets the score 2.0 requirements *and* responds correctly to the score 3.0 items.
Score 2.5	Student meets the score 2.0 requirements *and* responds partially correctly to the score 3.0 items.
Score 2.0	Student responds correctly to the score 2.0 item.
Score 1.5	Student responds partially correctly to the score 2.0 item.
Score 1.0	Student responds incorrectly to the score 2.0 item or needs help to answer.

Figure 5.10: Scoring guidance for grade 5 mathematics assessment.

Scoring Assessments That Include Multiple Proficiency Scales

There will no doubt be times when an assessment—most likely an end-of-cycle assessment—addresses multiple related proficiency scales. Standards are not always taught in isolation. In fact, in some content areas it is very common to address multiple standards simultaneously, resulting in assessments that address multiple proficiency scales. Consider a ninth-grade ELA instructional cycle that draws on three proficiency scales: (1) citing textual evidence, (2) ideas and themes, and (3) author's point of view, purpose, and use of rhetoric. Teachers must answer two important questions in relation to this instructional cycle.

1. What is the student's current level of performance on each proficiency scale included in the assessment?

2. What is the student's overall score on the assessment?

To discern the answer to these questions, teacher teams must design the assessment so that each assessment item relates to a specific level on one of the three scales and establish scoring guidance for each individual proficiency scale. Figure 5.11 provides important information about the number of items on the assessment for each scale and the scoring guidance.

Using this scoring guidance, it is easy for teachers to determine a final score for each proficiency scale. Consider the example student performance and scoring in figure 5.12. Having determined the student's score for each proficiency scale, the teacher can choose to stop here. The student will have three scores for this assessment, one for each topic. There is nothing wrong with this method, and some schools and districts prefer it. If the teacher wants to calculate an overall score for this assessment, however, there are several methods for combining the proficiency scale scores. One method is to average the scores; that is, add all three final scores together and then divide by three. In the case of the example in figure 5.12, $(2.5 + 2.0 + 1.5) \div 3 = 2.0$. This overall score of 2.0 suggests the student has acquired the foundational knowledge represented on the proficiency scales, but is not *yet* proficient on this group of scales.

Proficiency Scale	Number of Items on the Assessment	Scoring Guidance
Citing textual evidence	One score 2.0 item Two score 3.0 items One score 4.0 item	Score 2.0 = Only the score 2.0 item answered correctly Score 3.0 = Score 2.0 item and both score 3.0 items answered correctly Score 4.0 = All items answered correctly
Ideas and themes	Two score 2.0 items One score 3.0 items One score 4.0 item	Score 2.0 = Both score 2.0 items answered correctly Score 3.0 = Score 2.0 items and score 3.0 item answered correctly Score 4.0 = All items answered correctly
Author's point of view, purpose, and use of rhetoric	Two score 2.0 items Two score 3.0 items One score 4.0 item	Score 2.0 = Both score 2.0 items answered correctly Score 3.0 = Score 2.0 items and both score 3.0 items answered correctly Score 4.0 = All items answered correctly

Figure 5.11: Scoring guidance for assessment covering multiple proficiency scales, grade 9 ELA.

Citing textual evidence	Score 2.0: one out of one item correct Score 3.0: one out of two items correct Score 4.0: zero out of one item correct	Final score for citing textual evidence: 2.5
Ideas and themes	Score 2.0: two out of two items correct Score 3.0: zero out of one item correct Score 4.0: zero out of one item correct	Final score for ideas and themes: 2.0
Author's point of view, purpose, and use of rhetoric	Score 2.0: one out of two items correct Score 3.0: zero out of two items correct Score 4.0: zero out of one item correct	Final score for author's point of view, purpose, and rhetoric: 1.5

Figure 5.12: Sample student performance and scores for assessment covering multiple proficiency scales, grade 9 ELA.

Another method for determining an overall score works best when the assessment addresses multiple scales but only one scale level, such as only score 3.0 items related to two different scales. This method involves tallying the total number of items on the assessment, and then assigning ranges of correct answers to score values. Let's say an end-of-cycle assessment only includes score 3.0 items, two for each of three proficiency scales included in the cycle for a total of six items. The following information can be used to determine an overall score.

- Score 4.0: six items correct
- Score 3.0: five items correct
- Score 2.0: three or four items correct
- Score 1.0: one or two items correct

We do not recommend using this method when the assessment covers multiple scale levels because it does not consider the differing level of rigor associated with each item.

In summary, when an individual teacher or team of teachers determines scoring guidance prior to giving an assessment, the process of assigning an overall score is quite easy.

Determining a Final Grade

In a standards-based classroom, assessments based on proficiency scales not only provide information for teachers to make accurate decisions about student performance but also set the stage for standards-based reporting—giving students (and ultimately parents) information about their performance relative to standards. Traditionally, when it is time to report a grade, teachers have calculated an average percentage or letter grade. Standards-based learning suggests a different approach to determining a final grade. Grading and reporting are beyond the scope of this book, but we will provide a brief overview here. In a standards-based system, determining a final grade involves examining a pattern of proficiency scale scores from various assessments throughout a unit or grading period. Consider the set of scores in figure 5.13 for the second-grade mathematics instructional unit on telling time to the nearest five minutes.

Preassessment (score 2.0)	Telling Time to the Hour Worksheet (score 2.0)	Whiteboard Activity (score 3.0)	End-of-Cycle Assessment (score 4.0)	Final Grade
2.0	2.0	2.5	3.0	3.0

Figure 5.13: Pattern of proficiency scale scores.

Each assessment activity is indicated as a column heading, along with the highest score possible on the assessment. Notice that the first two assessments address only the score 2.0 content while the third and fourth assessments include the higher levels on the proficiency scale. The final grade is not an average of the assessment scores; instead, the teacher examined the student's pattern of performance to arrive at the decision of 3.0 as the final grade. The end-of-cycle assessment carries the most weight in the teacher's decision, as it is most recent and it reflects the point in time when students have engaged in the most learning. This type of decision making values students' learning over time and produces scores that accurately reflect their knowledge. It is appropriate in a standards-based learning environment because it provides information about performance relative to proficiency scales.

Summary

This chapter presents information about effective scoring of classroom assessments, in particular end-of-cycle assessments. Teachers must clearly understand how to score the different item types included on assessments, from selected-response items to constructed-response items and performance tasks. Finally, we present insights and methods for determining the final score on an assessment and using a collection of scores for making decisions about student performance. When teachers address scoring in a thoughtful way, accurate information about the degree of student learning is the outcome, which is no doubt the desire of every teacher who administers and scores classroom assessments!

Chapter 5 Reflection Questions

1. What is important to remember about scoring selected-response items?

2. How is scoring a constructed-response item different from scoring a selected-response item?

3. How is a rubric used when scoring a performance task?

4. How might a teacher determine a final score for an assessment?

5. Thinking of a unit you have taught or currently teach, how might you apply the concepts or strategies discussed in this chapter?

6

The Use of Data From Assessments

Key idea: Classroom assessment is the most immediate and common method teachers use to monitor learning. The data produced from classroom assessments provide valuable insight regarding necessary adjustments that educators may need to consider in the teaching and learning process.

Teachers do not give assessments for their own sake—their purpose is to provide information that teachers use to make informed decisions about student learning. If educators did not use the data assessments provide, they would waste a great deal of valuable time administering them. The high-quality assessment practices we have discussed so far generate critical data for teachers to apply as they move forward with instruction. A key premise of this book is to emphasize the concept of assessment as a teaching and learning tool. The data generated from assessments inform decisions that guide the teaching and learning processes in a standards-based learning environment. This chapter considers important matters related to what teachers should do after giving and scoring assessments. Specifically, the following sections address setting up for success, using data to plan instruction, analyzing achievement data, and tracking progress and setting goals.

Setting Up for Success

How might a teacher or team of teachers ensure their own success when using data in a standards-based classroom? This is a critical question, as every assessment offered to students has the potential to provide valuable information regarding how to improve current levels of learning. However, if teachers do not plan for success, data may have minimal positive impact on student learning. Educational consultants Laura Lipton and Bruce Wellman (2012) shared some tips for preparing for success with data analysis.

- Structure the workspace so it is conducive to reviewing information and having conversations. This may mean having tables during some portions of the review and chairs in a semicircle for engaging in deeper conversations.

- Provide time for all participants to become oriented to the data before asking for comments or questions. This provides time for each person to independently explore the data and make sense of them.

- Develop a process for looking at the information. For example, "We will start with our statewide results, and then we will move to our common assessment results."

- Apply structures and processes for balancing participation for all involved. It may help to assign a timekeeper, materials manager, recorder, and facilitator, for instance.

- Establish ways to publicly record the information. Will you use paper charts on the walls? Will you project spreadsheets?

- Record important data in clear and concise ways. Record both initial observations (assessment results) and final working conclusions.

- Depersonalize the information. Be certain teacher and student names are omitted to keep the analysis and conversations focused on the data and refrain from personal comments or defensiveness.

These processes help you set up and maintain effective data-analysis practices.

Using Data to Plan Instruction

As mentioned in chapter 3 (page 51), teachers should use data protocols to discuss assessment results with their teams and make decisions about future instruction. The data for discussion can derive from any assessment and should specifically look at concepts where student performance is strong as well as concepts where student performance needs improvement. In the data-discussion process, teachers identify common areas of misunderstanding or errors. Following this identification, teachers can plan to revisit these topics to ensure learners advance their understanding in relation to the standards.

Figure 6.1 represents a high school collaborative team's data protocol. Notice that it guides teachers to not only analyze the data from the previous assessment but also set goals to move forward. While the protocol is quite complex and detailed, it provides valuable information that helps the collaborative team engage in meaningful planning across the entire unit of instruction. It also helps to ensure that students' individual needs are met.

Some teams simply choose to follow a sequence of questions to use assessment data in a meaningful way. One simple set is as follows.

1. What can we learn from these data?

2. Do we have other data to support these results?

3. What are the implications of these data?

4. What actions will we take as a result of these data?

Grade level or subject: _____ Date: _____ Recorder: _____

Team members: _____

_____

Priority standards addressed: _____

_____

Learning targets from the proficiency scales (data comes from these): _____

_____

SMART (strategic and specific, measurable, attainable, results oriented, time bound) goal: ____ percent of all students will score at proficient or advanced on (learning targets), as measured by (assessment) given during the week of _____.

After reteaching and reassessing, ____ percent of those students below mastery level on the common assessment will be proficient or advanced.

____ percent of all students have demonstrated mastery. ____ percent of students have not. What are our plans for those students?

Procedure:

1. Record data.

2. Analyze strengths and needs.

3. Discuss what teaching strategies we used and identify what worked and what did not work.

4. Reference the following ideas and discuss additional ideas with the team.

- Comparing and contrasting
- Classifying
- Group structures
- Creating or using metaphors or analogies
- Cueing
- Graphic organizers
- Hypothesizing

- Homework
- Note taking
- Practice
- Feedback with practice
- Summarizing
- Other

What are other possible strategies to try? Select strategies we can control versus those like "Increase parent involvement" or "Student will ask teacher."

5. As a team, decide what we will use for the next common assessment and when we will give it.

6. Apply this work and teach the content.

Data point 1: List the common assessment used by all teammates.

Figure 6.1: Sample data protocol.

continued →

Teachers and class level	Number of total students	Number of students scoring proficient or advanced	Percent of students scoring proficient or advanced	Number of students scoring progressing	Percent of students scoring progressing	Number of students scoring beginning	Percent of students scoring beginning
Totals							

Did we reach our goal? Y or N

7. Analyze strengths and needs.

　• Do we notice any trends or patterns?

　• What teaching strategies did we use?

　• What might we try for students not meeting proficiency?

　• Other

8. Set a new SMART goal and repeat the process with additional data points.

Percentage of all students scoring at proficient or advanced will increase from ___ percent to ___ percent by _____ (date) as measured by _____ (assessment).

9. Summarize the entire process and record what worked well and what we will do differently next time we teach it.

Source: © 2016 by Kerstin L. Rowe & Kerrie Schultz. Adapted with permission.

Other teachers might choose to use this version.

1. What data are we reviewing?

2. What can we learn from them?

3. Do we have other data to support (or refute) this information?

4. What are the actions or implications for next steps?

The key is not in the review itself (although this is important) but in the actions for students. Looking at student-assessment data (from high-quality classroom assessments) provides teachers with the facts. For example, a team reviewing assessment data might recognize a pattern of students missing a key step in the process of solving a specific type of problem. The team plans for how they will revisit the concept in class, call specific attention to the common mistake, and reteach it. Likewise, a team could notice that all their students have achieved conceptual mastery of key concepts or processes they have taught. The team decides to deliberately call attention to this success to affirm student understanding of the concept. The use of assessment data to inform next steps empowers teachers to empower students to revise or affirm their knowledge and skills.

Developing an environment where using data to inform teaching and learning is the norm takes time. Figure 6.2 presents a survey that teams and schools can use to find out how individual teachers view the culture. Based on the results of a survey such as this, leaders can use the information to plan how to enhance the perception of the culture. Teacher teams can work diligently to respond positively to the culture enhancements that evolve.

Read each statement regarding the use of data. Circle the level that best reflects the culture of your collaborative team or school.						
Data are used to . . .	**LOW**				**HIGH**	**Notes**
Replace hunches and hypotheses with facts concerning necessary changes	1	2	3	4	5	
Identify the root causes of problems and work to solve the problems rather than dwell on symptoms	1	2	3	4	5	
Assess needs for more information	1	2	3	4	5	
Know that goals are being accomplished with evidence	1	2	3	4	5	
Understand the impact of efforts, processes, and initiatives	1	2	3	4	5	
Continuously improve all aspects of the organization	1	2	3	4	5	
Inform curriculum and instructional decisions	1	2	3	4	5	

Figure 6.2: Data culture survey.

*Visit **MarzanoResources.com/reproducibles** for a free reproducible version of this figure.*

Analyzing Achievement Data

To reiterate, it is not in the mere collection of data where educators make discoveries but rather in the deep analysis thereof. Examining data allows educators to identify where they need to focus their energy. As Victoria L. Bernhart (1998), a leader in using data to increase student learning, said, "Disaggregation is not a problem-solving strategy. It is a problem-finding strategy" (p. 27). There are four lenses through which to consider data analysis (Bernhart, 1998, 2004, 2018).

1. **Student learning data:** These include state or provincial exams, standardized assessments like the ACT or SAT, portfolios of student work, and even student grades.

2. **Demographic data:** These include free and reduced lunch information (as one determiner of poverty), parent education levels, student ethnicity, mobility rates, discipline referrals, suspensions and expulsions, daily attendance, and the like. These data sets help teachers understand which students are performing in which ways.

3. **Perceptual data:** These include school climate surveys; reviews of social media posts; volunteerism; student, teacher, and parent opinions; and so on. Perceptions are real unless they are proven otherwise.

4. **Program and process data:** These include class size, number of years of experience within the teaching staff, teacher-student ratios, enrollment rates for special education, multilingual learner programs, gifted and talented programs, and so on.

Bernhart (1998, 2004, 2018) suggested that educators look at the intersections of these data sets. In other words, drill down through different sets of data to find the potential crossovers that could be impacting student performance. The purpose is to find contributing factors that might be affecting learning. Asking questions using two- and three-way intersections of the various data sets provides areas to explore. For example, teachers might ask questions like the following.

- What primary language (demographic) do students who are underperforming on our common assessments (student achievement) speak?

- How do students in our special education programs (program and process) feel about school (perceptual)?

- How does attendance (demographic) impact scores on benchmark assessments (student achievement)?

The intersections are numerous, and they spark many ways to review and use data. There are various ways teachers can ask these questions. A practical way to start is to ask questions about overall performance by demographic groups first. One question might be, Is there a distinct difference in overall performance based on gender, ethnicity, socioeconomic status, or age of the learners? The next questions will arise from the answers to the first. For example, a team notices girls outperformed boys across all classrooms in which the team sampled data. This could trigger the team to ask, "What specific assessment items or tasks showed the widest disparity in performance between girls and boys?" or "Did the lower performance in boys include all demographic groups or was there a specific demographic group of boys that underperformed on specific items?" When exploring and answering these questions, teachers could also take Lipton and Wellman's (2012) suggestion to refine rough observations into refined observations. For example:

- Rough observation—"There is a downward performance trend from grade 5 to grade 7."

- Refined observation—"Thirty-eight percent of fifth graders were proficient compared to 12 percent of seventh graders." (Lipton & Wellman, 2012, p. 32)

The process of shifting from rough observations to refined observations is really a matter of adding specificity. The addition of specificity clarifies the next steps a team might need to take and what that action will entail. In the preceding example, the rough observation indicates there is a downward trend performance from grades 5 to 7 and the refined observation is the specific percentages reflected in that downward trend. These data can be refined even further by asking which specific aspects of performance carried the most weight in the downward trend. Once teachers have identified those aspects, they can take action to remediate the specific areas that contributed to the trend and prevent that downward trend in the future. Using the information is the key to monitoring successes and identifying challenges for change.

There is no one right way to analyze your student achievement results. Rather, review the example forms and processes shared and select a starting place for you and your team. What is reasonable? As you grow in your analysis skills, you will review more information and continue to make instructional decisions based on sound information.

Tracking Progress and Setting Goals

Tracking students' progress and setting goals for their growth is one of the most important uses of classroom assessment data. In this section, we emphasize student involvement in these processes. Keeping track of their own progress and setting their own goals helps students take ownership of their learning and allows them to see how they are moving toward mastery of the priority standards. For example, a student who is tracking her growth in writing recognizes that she needs to improve her use of quotes in the writing process. Knowing this empowers her to set a goal related to this learning target and take steps to strengthen her writing skills. As always, proficiency scales and the corresponding classroom assessments are the basis for these recommendations. Proficiency scales identify the progression of learning for students and assessments matched to specific levels of the scale provide learners with clarity on their own progression in the learning.

Tracking Progress

Students tracking their own progress is a key component of a standards-based classroom. When students track their progress using proficiency scales and classroom assessments, it empowers them to monitor and own their learning journey (Fisher & Frey, 2007; Heflebower et al., 2019; Marzano, 2017). When learners engage in classroom assessment practices, "Students understand how test scores and grades relate to their status on the progression of knowledge they are expected to master" (Marzano, 2017, p. 5). There are many ways to implement this practice in the classroom, requiring varying amounts of class time. A teacher may begin by carving out small amounts of time to share proficiency scales with students and have them track their knowledge and skills by simply circling or highlighting the different learning targets on the scale. At the beginning of the instructional cycle, the teacher gives all students a copy of the scale for the unit, and individual students indicate which targets they already know and which they do not in contrasting colors. The class repeats this process midway through the instructional cycle and again at the end. Students can compare the three copies of the scale from different points in the unit for an easy visualization of their progress. This process only takes fifteen or twenty total minutes throughout the unit.

Another useful practice is for teachers to share classroom assessment results with students to help them verify their progress with assessment evidence. After each check for understanding during an instructional cycle, teachers can briefly review the scored assessments with students. Students can correlate the assessment items to the learning targets on the scale as they highlight the ones they have mastered (as shown by the assessment). This should only take about ten minutes, and might occur four or five times per unit.

Students can also use a *personal tracking matrix* (Marzano, Norford, Finn, & Finn, 2017) to chart their progress throughout a unit. Using a tracking tool such as a personal tracking matrix can be something a teacher has the whole class do together or individual students can do it on their own. Both are effective and time efficient and shouldn't take more than a few minutes each time students are asked to do this. Figure 6.3 is a sample of a third-grade student tracking her progress based on various assessment tools used to check her understanding. The priority standards appear at the left, and each row has spaces for her to record assessment scores. The last column prompts her to identify how much gain she has made on each learning target, highlighting the importance of growth. Notice that in the last row, the student was already proficient on the preassessment and confirmed that score at the first check for understanding. This student therefore did not need to be assessed again on this standard.

Standard	Preassessment	Check for Understanding	Check for Understanding	Gain
	September 14	September 18	September 22	
I can use place value to round whole numbers to the nearest 10. (3.NBT.1)	2.0	2.5	3.0	1 scale point
I can use place value to round whole numbers to the nearest 100. (3.NBT.1)	2.0	2.0	2.0	No gain yet
I can fluently add up to 1,000 using various strategies. (3.NBT.2)	2.0	3.0	2.5	.5 scale point
I can fluently subtract up to 1,000 using various strategies. (3.NBT.2)	3.0	3.0		Proficient!

Source: Adapted from Heflebower et al., 2021.

Figure 6.3: Sample personal tracking matrix, grade 3 mathematics.

Another approach to a personal tracking matrix is to use student-friendly versions of the learning targets and break down more complex targets into discrete elements (Marzano, 2018). Figure 6.4 displays an example. Note that the learning targets use approachable language and each one has its own row so students can rate their progress on each target (including each vocabulary term) separately.

Standard RL.8.3—Analyzing Narrative—Eighth-Grade ELA					
Level	**Learning Target**	**My Rating**			**My Evidence**
		I'm still confused about this topic.	I've learned some but not all of this topic.	I've got this now.	
Level 4 (Advanced)	I can analyze the narratives of two different stories and compare and contrast the character development and theme within the different stories.				
Level 3 (Proficient)	I can analyze how elements of a story interact and shape the story.				
Level 3 (Proficient)	I can analyze how the author builds or reveals the lesson or theme found in a narrative.				
Level 2 (Progressing)	I can describe how the author uses characterization to build characters' personalities.				
Level 2 (Progressing)	I can summarize the events of the plot.				
Level 2 (Progressing)	I can determine a main conflict or problem for the character in a narrative.				
Level 2 (Progressing)	I can note descriptive details and sensory language to capture the action and experiences.				
Level 2 (Progressing)	I can describe the term *perspective*.				
Level 2 (Progressing)	I can describe the term *characterization*.				
Level 2 (Progressing)	I can describe the term *theme*.				
Level 2 (Progressing)	I can describe the term *narrative*.				
Level 2 (Progressing)	I can describe the term *sequence of events*.				

Source for standard: NGA & CCSSO, 2010a.

Source: Adapted from Marzano & Abbott, 2022.

Figure 6.4: Sample student-friendly personal tracking matrix, grade 8 ELA.

Figure 6.5 (page 112) offers another example of a personal tracking matrix. This version incorporates goal setting (which we discuss in the next section, page 112) and a visual graph. Teachers might also use a version of this chart to visually represent the progress of the class as a whole. The teacher could chart the average proficiency scale score or the percentage of students who have demonstrated proficiency over the course of the instructional cycle. This provides students a sense of how they are doing compared to others in an anonymous manner.

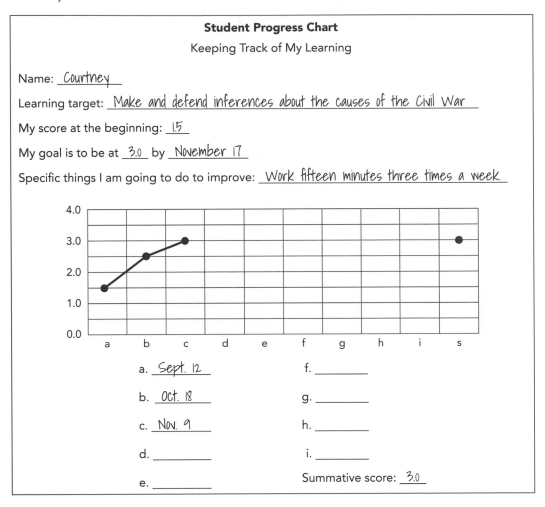

Source: Heflebower et al., 2019, p. 65.

Figure 6.5: Student progress chart.

Goal Setting

Once teachers have a strong understanding of assessment results, they can share individual student results with those students and engage them in the process of setting learning goals. Goal setting goes hand in hand with tracking progress. It takes time to implement student goal setting in the classroom, yet it can be a powerful process to increase student engagement in their own learning. In *A Teacher's Guide to Standards-Based Learning*, Heflebower and her colleagues (2019) stated:

> Goal setting is an integral part of a standards-based learning environment because it helps focus students on individual needs related to specific learning targets, and because the most important and influential instructional decisions are often made by learners themselves (Stiggins, 2008). Goal setting and tracking progress go hand in hand. As students set goals, they track progress about those standards-based learning targets. In turn,

> tracking progress provides students with information regarding their initial goals, and often will assist them in modifying the goal or creating a new one. (p. 47)

Since goal setting can influence learning in a positive way, we present a few steps for helping students set personal goals.

1. Provide assessment results for students so they know their current level of performance on the proficiency scales.

2. Provide a template for the goal-setting process. A goal-setting template may include the topic, the current score, the desired score, and how the student intends to attain the goal. A student learning goal using this template might read, "We are learning about force, energy, and motion in science. My current score on our scale for this topic is 2.0. My personal goal is a score of 3.0. I will attain this goal by participating in class discussion, engaging in class activities, and asking questions when I don't understand."

3. Engage students in tracking their progress toward their goals (discussed in the previous section, page 107).

4. Provide support and encouragement to students throughout the learning opportunity. For example, when students provide evidence to substantiate gain on the scale, affirm their efforts. Encourage additional effort in order to ensure that they meet their goals.

Just as the goal-setting process can foster success in many aspects of life—fitness, productivity, task accomplishment—it can work similarly in a standards-based classroom.

Summary

The point of giving assessment opportunities is to gain information about what students know and can do relative to the standards. This empowers teachers to utilize that information to adjust instruction and ensure all students learn. This chapter discussed several facets of using classroom assessment data to enhance standards-based learning. First, teachers need to have productive conversations about assessment results that allow them to plan for future instruction. Next, they can also delve deeply into achievement, demographic, perceptual, and process data to identify areas of success and opportunities for change. Finally, educators should involve students in the use of assessment data to generate ownership of their learning. Students should track their progress and set goals based on proficiency scales. In the next and final chapter, we consider another crucial way that teachers and students interact in the standards-based classroom: feedback.

Chapter 6 Reflection Questions

1. What is the purpose of assessment data in the standards-based classroom?

2. How should teachers enact the results of a data protocol discussion?

3. What is one question you could ask about your classroom or school using the intersections of student learning data, demographic data, perceptual data, and program and process data?

4. What are two strategies for students tracking their own progress and setting their own goals? Why are these practices important?

5. Thinking of a unit you have taught or currently teach, how might you apply the concepts or strategies discussed in this chapter?

7

Feedback to Students

Key idea: Understanding quality feedback strategies and using them to increase student achievement are critical for teachers in a standards-based learning system.

Quality feedback is an essential element of a standards-based classroom. In fact, some would argue feedback is more important than scores obtained (Brookhart, 2017; Hattie, 2012; Wiliam, 2011). Certainly, scores alone do not give students the information they need to increase their learning. Therefore, this chapter considers important matters related to the components of quality feedback paired with practical strategies for teachers to help students learn more.

The idea that students need feedback to excel may seem self-evident, but executing that idea in the classroom may take more intentional effort than one expects. Most teachers perceive they give a great deal of feedback to students. Educational assessment expert David Carless (2006) found that when surveyors "asked students and teachers whether teachers provided detailed feedback that helped students improve their next assignments, about 70 percent of teachers claimed they provided such detailed feedback often or always, but only 45 percent of students agreed with their teachers' claims" (as cited in Hattie, 2009, p. 174). In fact, teaching and learning scholar Graham Nuthall (2005) noted most of the feedback students received "was from other students, and most of this feedback was incorrect" (as cited in Hattie, 2009, p. 174).

One way to account for the discrepancy in the perception of teachers and students about the amount of feedback provided to them may concern the method by which teachers provide the feedback. Students want—and will often tell teachers they want—substantial feedback. Yet when teachers write voluminous comments on an assignment or assessment, students often glance at it or do not even read the feedback at all. Teachers also find that they are writing similar, if not the same, comments on assessment after assessment. Students may not see the connection between a comment made by a teacher and the changes they should make to correct those errors. In a standards-based learning environment, where learning goals and their associated proficiency scales are the basis of all instruction, assessment, and feedback, students are more likely to see the relevance of teacher feedback to their learning progression and be more amenable to quality feedback that will help them obtain their learning goals.

There are many reviews of feedback and suggestions for improving it (for example, Brooks, Carroll, Gillies, & Hattie, 2019; Hattie & Zierer, 2019; Wisniewski, Zierer, & Hattie, 2020). One early study of feedback, and one of the most notable, analyzed the degree to which different types of feedback engender gains (or losses) in student achievement (Bangert-Drowns, Kulik, Kulik, & Morgan, 1991). Table 7.1 summarizes those findings. Note that the largest positive effects come when students understand the assessment criteria, when the teacher explains the feedback, and when students are reassessed until they are correct.

Table 7.1: Feedback Studies

Type of Feedback	Number of Studies Analyzed	Student Achievement Gain or Loss
Teacher marks responses right or wrong.	6	–3 percent
Teacher provides corrected answers.	39	8.5 percent
Students understand the assessment criteria.	30	16 percent
Teacher explains feedback.	9	20 percent
Teacher reassesses students until correct.	4	20 percent

Source: Adapted from Bangert-Drowns et al., 1991.

Clearly, when feedback is part of the learning process in the form of explanations, reassessment, and ensuring students understand the criteria for success, student achievement gains strength. Researchers have continued to concur with this finding. Education scholars and authors Benedikt Wisniewski, Klaus Zierer, and John Hattie (2020) emphasized that feedback's efficacy varies depending on its content; feedback containing more information is superior to that simply sharing a raw score or percentage. Feedback that informs students about the task, the process, and the students' self-regulation level showed large effects (Wisniewski et al., 2020). Another notable feature is appropriate timing of feedback and its explicit relationship to what students are learning (Hattie & Timperley, 2007). All this is to say that students benefit most from feedback when it helps them understand any mistakes made, why they made them, and how to prevent them in the future.

Proficiency scales that serve as the basis of instruction and assessment provide assessment criteria that students can easily understand and meet the preceding criteria for what makes more effective feedback. We also advocate for multiple assessments of student performance—in other words, reassessing students until they demonstrate understanding of the content on a proficiency scale. This chapter explores specific aspects of direct, well-explained feedback that helps students learn and then provides practical ideas for integrating feedback into the instructional cycle.

Considerations for Quality Feedback

High-quality feedback is an essential part of the learning process, and done well, it has a notable impact. Hattie (2009) defined feedback as "information provided by an agent (e.g., teacher, peer, book, parent, or one's own experience) about aspects of one's performance or understanding" (p. 174). Brookhart (2017) reiterated that point when she stated, "Effective feedback is part of a classroom assessment environment in which students see constructive criticism as a good thing and understand that learning cannot occur without practice" (p. 9). Effective feedback is information provided to complement, enhance, augment, or in some way respond to or improve performance.

Sufficient and effective feedback is more about quality than quantity. Based on our review of the literature, the following characteristics make feedback higher quality and more useful to students (Brookhart, 2017; Carless, 2006; Hattie, 2009; Hattie & Timperley, 2007; Hattie & Zierer, 2019; Nuthall, 2005; Wisniewski et al., 2020).

- **Clarity:** It is easy to understand what the feedback is suggesting for improvement.

- **Focus on the task, process, or self-regulation:** The feedback focuses on the assignment or how the student engaged in the assignment.

- **Specificity:** The feedback addresses something specific about the quality of the task or the student's engagement in the task.

- **Tone:** The feedback is constructive and communicated in a way that fosters receptiveness.

- **Timeliness:** The feedback is offered in proximity to the task.

- **Appropriate methods:** Feedback is offered in such a way that it can be used effectively. This feedback may be verbal or written.

- **Consideration of the audience:** The language of the feedback is appropriate for the receiver.

- **Amount:** The amount of feedback does not overwhelm the receiver and provides actionable tasks for improvement.

- **Comparison to criteria:** Suggestions for improvement are based on the learning targets on the proficiency scales.

For our purposes, we focus on five components from this list: (1) specificity, (2) tone, (3) timeliness, (4) amount, and (5) comparison to criteria (that is, the proficiency scale). These are most relevant to a standards-based learning environment.

Specificity

Specificity relates to including enough detail that students know what to do to improve their work. Imagine a middle school student who receives feedback saying, "Please be more methodical in your lab write-up." The student would likely be confused because "be more methodical" is not very specific feedback and is therefore not actionable. In fact, the student might respond by saying, "I would be more methodical if I knew what that meant or how to do that." More specific feedback might sound like, "Please use the parts of your lab setup and results sections to justify your thinking. Tell me more about what you did and what you found out. Use procedures, numbers, graphs, and descriptive statements."

Additionally, teachers may use questions, prompts, and cues to help students think about errors. Instead of saying things like "You need to show your work," a teacher could give a prompt or cue like, "When you explain your thinking in words, I know what you are doing. For example, show me with arrows or brackets that you multiplied 7×3, instead of simply putting 21 near the problem." This type of feedback includes examples of what will help students be successful, rather than assuming they know what the teacher means by "show your work."

Provide just enough feedback to get the student redirected or moving ahead (Saphier, 2005). The feedback you provide students should be detailed yet not so verbose that students do not need to think. If a student says, "I don't get what you mean," your response might be, "Let's look back at the problem you did previously. What do you notice about it? How might this help you with this new problem? I'll check back with you, and let's see what you can discover first." Perhaps the best advice is to approach feedback in narrowly focused chunks, aligned to the learning goals around which you designed the activity or assessment, so students can work on specific knowledge or skills related to these learning goals.

Proficiency scales assist in giving specific feedback because teachers can reference particular learning targets when discussing students' knowledge and skills. For example, teachers can easily reference the proficiency scale and specific learning targets to denote (perhaps even physically underlining, circling, or highlighting) which elements of content need attention. This increases the specificity of the feedback for the student.

Tone

Be sure the tone you want to convey is the tone that comes through in your feedback. We suggest being honest, specific, and kind. Be mindful of how the student receiving the feedback perceives it. You want a student to see feedback as helpful, not as overly critical. Feedback with a harsh or negative tone can cause the emotional centers of students' brains to flare up and prevent them from responding rationally—even if the content of the feedback is useful (Feinstein, 2006). As Brookhart (2008) noted, "Tone can inspire or discourage. It's important to choose words that imply that students are agents, active learners—the captains of their own ship of learning, as it were" (p. 34). This does not mean to sugarcoat descriptive feedback. Be honest. Provide suggestions. But moderate your tone for the best results.

Take the time to thoughtfully phrase your feedback. Instead of using curt phrases like, "More details! This doesn't make sense," try, "More details will enhance your point. I am not sure about the meaning of this statement, and more information would help me understand better." Then, reread your feedback from the student's point of view. You can also seek input from students about how they receive your feedback. Check in with students through journals or verbal conversations to ensure they have interpreted the feedback as intended. Alternatively, ask students to summarize your feedback in their own terms to monitor their understanding and interpretation of the tone.

Feedback should not be limited to corrections. Provide specific comments on strengths as well. Even a simple statement like, "Your introduction clearly states what I am going to be reading about" helps balance the overall tone of the comments. Consider providing feedback about attributes students may be exhibiting. For instance, if students can track their effort on an assignment as well as how they achieved, they discover how their efforts relate to results. Providing feedback to students about the amount or type of effort they exhibited on the assignment may help students see the connection between behavior and achievement and encourage them to repeat beneficial behaviors in the future.

We also suggest that, in a standards-based classroom, using the proficiency scale as the basis of feedback makes students more likely to perceive teacher feedback as constructive. If the students' focus is on the learning progression and not on the score, students will see teacher comments as helping them move along the learning progression of the scale. This assumes, of course, that the tone of these comments is constructive, warm, engaging, and helpful. Making the proficiency scale the centerpiece of the feedback discussion helps students view the teacher's comments more objectively.

Finally, it is important to note that teachers must be mindful of the classroom culture and climate they cultivate. As one might imagine, when the culture of the classroom is one of mutual respect, students are more likely to receive and provide feedback in positive ways. If the classroom culture is one where feedback is perceived as critical and personal, students may disregard it. Foster an environment that encourages students and teachers to use feedback.

Timeliness

There are several aspects to the timeliness of feedback. The first is to provide feedback at pivotal points in the learning process. Allow students time to grapple with an idea a bit before jumping in with a great deal of corrective feedback. According to formative assessment expert Dylan Wiliam (2018), "if [feedback] is given too early, before students have had a chance to work on a problem, then they will learn less" (p. 127). Teachers might use more questions than statements to give feedback early in the learning process. For example, a music teacher could ask, "Can you tell me what you heard while playing that measure?" Later in the learning journey, feedback might sound like, "How did you improve your performance throughout the piece?"

The second aspect of timeliness is returning assignments in a reasonable time frame to provide feedback as close to the learning as possible. Students benefit less from feedback when there is too much of a delay between completing the assessment or assignment and receiving feedback on that work (Bangert-Drowns et al., 1991; Brookhart, 2017). It is important to note that a reasonable time frame may vary by assignment. It should be relatively easy for teachers to provide prompt feedback on short quizzes and exit tickets, for example. Technology tools can be useful in sharing feedback quickly. For example, tools like clickers and online surveys compile individual and classwide results almost instantly.

But students also need to receive timely feedback on more complex assignments. For instance, if a student turns in an essay and does not receive any feedback for two weeks, the student might forget the learning related to that essay and perceive that it was not important. Even when complete, in-depth feedback takes more time, if a teacher can spot-check a couple of key paragraphs or assessment items, the student can receive some sort of feedback sooner and more efficiently. Shared documents (such as Google Docs) allow teachers to leave comments on essays, recorded performances, and other extended responses that students can view in real time.

Yet another essential characteristic of timeliness is ensuring that students have time to react to the feedback prior to the final evaluation of the work. Feedback on a traditional final exam is quite pointless. When students have opportunities to do something with the feedback in a formative manner, it is valuable. If teachers wait for a summative assessment to give feedback with little or no opportunity for students to make modifications, feedback may be a moot point. There is no opportunity for students to make corrections or modify their understanding. Sports coaches often model feedback that allows for adjustment. For example, a volleyball coach who observes a player making an error would provide correction and modeling and then ask the player to perform five or ten repetitions of the corrected skill. This correction with practice helps ensure the player has time to incorporate the feedback so the accurate practice becomes permanent. Allow students to use the feedback provided and adjust their performance accordingly.

The final aspect of timeliness is that the timing of appropriate feedback may vary from student to student. At the secondary level, we recommend allowing student choice in this matter. For example, during a weeklong project, a teacher could tell students that each person can receive one teacher feedback session; each student decides at what point this might be most helpful. Some students may want feedback early in the process to ensure they are on the right track. Others might hold off on the teacher feedback opportunity until after receiving feedback from a peer and revising their project accordingly. In an elementary setting, student-by-student variation would likely be more teacher-directed. Imagine a teacher checking on students' progress with a mathematics problem. The teacher may check in once with each student, starting with more advanced students. This way, the teacher can quickly check in on students who typically need less assistance, moving them ahead. Then, the teacher may use the remainder of the time conducting minilessons for those exhibiting need of more intensive observations and feedback.

Amount

Keeping the amount of feedback focused and reasonable is an important consideration so as not to overwhelm students. The first strategy we suggest is to select a couple of main points for comments rather than commenting on everything. Think triage—in an emergency room, medical professionals treat a person's most serious injury or illness first. When reviewing a student's work, ask, "What is the most significant aspect warranting feedback?" Once again, clearly articulated learning goals and proficiency scales will help narrow the focus and amount of feedback. For instance, if a student demonstrates misunderstanding of one of the learning targets on a proficiency scale, that warrants feedback. Conversely, if a student makes a small conventional or computational mistake (less significant in the bigger picture), a teacher may not provide as much feedback about such an error.

Another approach is to focus on conceptual errors rather than on simple mistakes. Correcting every single mistake is not only exhausting for the teacher but also frustrating for the student. Rather, professors Douglas Fisher and Nancy Frey (2012) suggested, "Correcting mistakes while failing to address errors can be a costly waste of instructional time." The difference between mistakes and errors is that mistakes occur through a lack of attention while errors "occur because of a lack of knowledge" (Fisher & Frey, 2012). To improve student learning, teachers should focus feedback on the places where students lack knowledge or skill. There are four types of errors (Fisher & Frey, 2012).

1. *Factual errors* are about accuracy. Students may not understand a key concept and make errors in understanding a term.

2. *Procedural errors* are those in misapplying a skill. Students may fail to use the order of operations as intended. They may add prior to multiplying in an equation, for instance.

3. *Application errors* involve applying information to the wrong situation. Students may overgeneralize a characteristic to an entire population or use a process in an unrelated context.

4. *Misconception errors* are those where students think certain things because the contrary is counterintuitive. For example, students may think we have seasons because Earth moves closer to and farther away from the sun, since they know as you get closer to a heat source, the temperature is warmer. However, the misconception is that students do not clearly understand Earth's tilt on its axis while revolving around the sun.

Focusing on big-picture errors saves teachers time in marking every single mistake, some of which may be insignificant.

It is also helpful to look for patterns in a student's errors and make an effort to determine the knowledge that student is missing (Fisher & Frey, 2012). In the standards-based classroom, when teachers reference the important content and skills on proficiency scales, they can see exactly where students are making errors and work to correct them. What is the common error? If students continue to balance chemical equations incorrectly, is it due to a lack of clarity about protons, neutrons, and electrons? If students are continually misusing contractions, do they not understand what a contraction does? Do they confuse what letters the apostrophe replaces? Looking for patterns in this way, teachers can provide effective feedback about students' knowledge and understanding rather than noting singular errors. It also enables teachers to identify groups of students who have similar misunderstandings and saves the time of writing all the same comments for each student yet provides the specificity and timeliness of the feedback to students in a personal format.

Comparison to Criteria

By using proficiency scales and their corresponding classroom assessments as the foundation for quality feedback, teachers can objectively signify strengths and challenges about student products or processes. Criterion-referenced feedback that compares students' progress to a clearly identified set of knowledge and skills (that is, the priority standards) is preferable to comparing students to one another. That latter type of norm-referenced feedback encourages students to imitate successful students or, worse, makes some students give up in fear they can never be like others. Compare students to themselves (that is, monitor their growth) or to a set of criteria (that is, a proficiency scale).

When teachers use proficiency scales for instruction and feedback, students have a framework within which to place critical comments. Students are familiar with the learning progression used during instruction, and they know where they are on that progression because the assessments are aligned to the scale. Thus, when teachers provide feedback in terms of the scale, students access their background knowledge about the scale. If students have set personal goals relative to the proficiency scale, they will view the teachers' comments as useful for working toward their goals. All this contextual support provided by the proficiency scale better equips students to apply the criticism in the next assignment.

Of course, asking students to respond to critical feedback in terms of the proficiency scale takes instruction and modeling. It is important that teachers explain how to use the scale for critical feedback, the reasoning that students should apply to understand the critical comments in terms of the scale, and the next steps that students should take after receiving and reading the criticism. Teachers should also encourage students to seek additional information from the teacher if they are confused or unsure about how to apply the criticism in terms of the proficiency scale.

Additionally, students can self-reflect on their learning journeys, redirecting and revising work based on the use of a proficiency scale and corresponding classroom assessments. Often, students can use these proficiency scales to engage parents in the conversation about their learning progress. Teachers can even use proficiency scales during parent-teacher conferences. This leads to engaging conversations with parents and students around an objective set of criteria about which the student demonstrated strengths and weaknesses. Not only does this make the conversation more productive, but it also keeps the focus on learning rather than the accumulation of points toward a percentage or letter grade (the traditional grading models parents might expect).

Practical Ideas for Integrating Feedback

There are many ideas for regularly integrating feedback into the standards-based classroom. In this section, we detail practical ideas for making feedback less time intensive for teachers yet meaningful for students.

Feedback During the Instructional Cycle

To begin, it is important to understand how to discuss the proficiency scale that serves as the basis of an instructional cycle with students. What should teachers say? How is feedback with a scale different from traditional classroom feedback? We explore these questions through an extended example including dialogues with students related to proficiency scales.

Imagine a fifth-grade class beginning an instructional cycle on fractions. The proficiency scale for this unit appears in figure 7.1. To understand the feedback that a teacher would provide to students in this example, we must identify the specific learning targets within the scale.

Score 4.0	In addition to score 3.0, in-depth inference and applications that go beyond instruction to the standard
Score 3.5	In addition to scores 3.0 performance, in-depth inferences and applications with partial success
Score 3.0	The student will: • Solve word problems involving the addition and subtraction of fractions referring to the same whole, including cases of unlike denominators • Use benchmark fractions to estimate answers and check for reasonableness
Score 2.5	No major errors or omissions regarding 2.0 content and partial knowledge of the 3.0 content and skills
Score 2.0	There are no major errors or omissions regarding the simpler details and processes as the student will: Recognize or recall specific vocabulary such as *benchmark fractions* and *mixed numbers* The student will perform basic processes, such as: • Identify the lowest common denominator of two fractions • Add fractions with unlike denominators including mixed numbers • Subtract fractions with unlike denominators including mixed numbers However, the student exhibits major errors or omissions regarding the more complex ideas and processes
Score 1.0	With help, a partial understanding of the 2.0 content, but major errors or omissions regarding the 3.0 content and processes
Score 0.5	With help, a partial understanding of the 2.0 content, but not the 3.0 content
Score 0.0	Even with help, no understanding or skill demonstrated

Source: Adapted from Marzano et al., 2013.

Figure 7.1: Proficiency scale for word problems with fractions, grade 5 mathematics.

This scale represents a learning progression based on two priority standards for fifth-grade mathematics standards.

1. The student will solve word problems involving the addition and subtraction of fractions referring to the same whole, including cases of unlike denominators.

2. The student will use benchmark fractions to estimate answers and check for reasonableness.

Students will work to achieve score 3.0 proficiency on both standards during the cycle. Early in the unit, the class will focus on the score 2.0 content, such as vocabulary, adding and subtracting fractions, and identifying and using the lowest common denominator.

The teacher will start the instructional cycle by providing direct instruction on the proficiency scale itself. Throughout the unit, a student-friendly version of the proficiency scale is available and on display in the classroom. Although feedback will change slightly as the cycle evolves, we shall examine ways in which teachers can connect students with the proficiency scales at the start of the unit and use the students' knowledge of proficiency scales to effectively deliver feedback later on.

At the start of the first lesson on the process of finding the lowest common denominator, the teacher might refer to the proficiency scale and ask students to self-rate their status on understanding and being able to use the process. Most students will likely score themselves low on the scale, at or below score 2.0. As students learn or review the foundational skill of finding the lowest common denominator, the teacher shares the steps of the process, and students engage in guided practice in class. Often, the first independent work comes in the form of homework, though independent work in class is also an option. These initial efforts are not graded or recorded in the gradebook, as students are in the early stages of learning the content. Instead, the teacher collects and evaluates the work, returning it as part of the feedback students receive about their learning. Sometimes a teacher goes over the work in class, having students score their own work and offering an opportunity for them to ask questions during this time. Other times, the teacher might provide time for students to review their work independently and self-assess their strengths and challenges in relation to the proficiency scale. In either case, the basis of the feedback is the proficiency scale.

After the teacher scores the initial independent work, the teacher asks students to return to the proficiency scale:

> Now that we have had a chance to practice the steps in finding lowest common denominators, let's take another look at the proficiency scale and decide what progress we've made. Take a moment to remember your first score, the one you gave yourself when we started. Now, consider the work you've done, consider how well you think you're understanding and using the process, and rate yourself on the scale again. Now, everyone put your heads down, and when I say go, please show me with your fingers what score you would give yourself now. Would you be a 2.0? That would mean you know the steps and can use them well. Would you be a 3.0? That would mean you can use those steps in hard fraction problems! Or would you be at a 1.0? That would mean you still need a little help from me to do the process. Remember, no one will see the score but you and me. OK, go.

Students then indicate with their fingers where they see themselves. This kind of self-rating keeps students aware of the progress they are making and of what their next steps in the learning progression will likely be, in terms of the proficiency scale.

Further, the activity represents an effective form of instructional feedback to the teacher since the teacher can look around the room and understand where the students see themselves on the learning progression. The teacher will directly assess students more in the future, but students' judgments of their own progress can be surprisingly accurate if they are familiar with the proficiency scale. Having received this instructional feedback, the teacher can judge next steps for the students. If the students feel they are making progress and the teacher's impressions support that, the class will proceed to the next level of learning in the proficiency scale or a more formal assessment. If the teacher feels it is necessary, it might be time for additional review or reteaching to help the students solidify the skill of the lowest common denominator process and its application.

As the cycle proceeds, students will encounter assessments that provide the teacher with specific data on each student's progress. An assessment that covers all three levels on a proficiency scale is very useful for determining the position of each student on the proficiency scale. After students complete this assessment and the teacher has scored it and returned students' work for them to look through, the teacher has another opportunity for feedback in terms of the proficiency scale. Ideally, such feedback takes two forms: (1) general feedback to the entire class and (2) specific feedback to individual students. The teacher might say to the class:

> In looking at our scores on this assessment, a couple of things seem clear. As a class, we are making our way up the proficiency scale. Let's look at the scale. We started below level 2.0, learning the steps to finding lowest common denominator. As a class, our overall performance is at 2.8, which means we not only understand the steps in the process, but we're also able to use it correctly with lots of different kinds of problems. That is really good progress as a class! Now, some of us might be a little ahead of that progress, and some are still working at reaching that level, but overall, we're doing well! Give yourselves a pat on your back. You're doing a great job!

At the same time, individual students need to understand their own status on the proficiency scale, identifying the progress they have made and the next steps. When students have received their scored assessments back, they should record their scores on their progress-tracking forms. At this time, the teacher can also move desk to desk to discuss individual progress with each student. Such conversations are typically brief, but some students may need a longer opportunity to discuss their own progress.

> Teacher: *I see that you have recorded the score from our last assessment on lowest common denominators on your tracking sheet. What does the tracking sheet tell you about your progress?*
>
> Student: *Well, I started off low, and then the score got higher and higher. At one point, I was at 2.5, but on the last assessment, my score went down to 2.0. I thought I was doing well, but it looks like I'm getting worse!*
>
> Teacher: *Let's look at the assessment for a moment. As you look it over, what did you do well?*
>
> Student: *I got most of the steps in the process right. It was just on the harder problems at 3.0 that I didn't do so well.*
>
> Teacher: *When we went over those problems in class, could you see what you did wrong?*
>
> Student: *Yes. In three problems, I multiplied the denominators wrong. I don't know how I did that.*
>
> Teacher: *What will you do next time to avoid that?*
>
> Student: *I think I need to slow down a little to make sure I do each step correctly.*
>
> Teacher: *Good! That's a good idea to focus on next time to see if you can get that score back up to 2.5 or maybe 3.0.*

Importantly, the student identifies the problem and a potential solution.

Throughout the cycle of instruction, students can celebrate their success and identify how to achieve the next level of the scale. The focus of feedback is on the learning, not the score. This is an important difference in standards-based learning, and using feedback in this manner has the effect of shifting students' focus away from the grade and onto the learning.

As you can see by this example, the proficiency scale should take center stage in these discussions, as it should during instruction itself. Because students will focus on the learning goals for the unit, the discussion in terms of the proficiency scale both supports and deepens that focus. Indeed, as we have indicated throughout this book, the proficiency scale is the element that ties together all the interaction between teacher and student in a standards-based classroom.

Personalized Feedback

Feedback is best when it is personalized. While general feedback to a whole class has its place (as exemplified in the previous section), a teacher would rarely provide content-specific feedback to the entire class, unless, of course, everyone in the class made the same errors. Rather, teachers consider whether feedback applies to a small group (students who made similar mistakes or are in the same place in their learning) or to individual students.

In most cases, personalized feedback is more meaningful to students. This might sound more effort intensive for teachers, but there are many ways to enact personalized feedback efficiently. It is not necessary to have frequent, extended one-on-one meetings with every student. Brookhart (2017) mentioned a strategy called *quick-and-quiet feedback*, which she described as "individual, extemporaneous feedback provided to students when you notice a need" (p. 51). For example, a teacher who is monitoring independent practice might notice a student who looks stuck. The teacher might whisper, "What do you recall about the sample on the whiteboard? Does your setup begin like the example?" Sometimes words are not even needed; perhaps a teacher simply points to part of a procedure a student needs to attend to without saying anything at all. Personalizing feedback is essential for students to monitor their learning and make adjustments.

Feedback on Student Products

While some classroom feedback is verbal, teachers often provide written feedback on students' assessments, written work, and other work products. As alluded to in our discussion of the appropriate amount of feedback (page 120), it is often better to prompt students to seek their own errors and take corrective action than to correct every minor mistake. Wiliam (2011) reminded us, "If I had to reduce all of the research on feedback into one simple overarching idea, at least for academic subjects in school, it would be this: feedback should cause thinking" (p. 127). Brookhart (2017) suggested writing guiding questions in the margins, such as the following.

- "Can you add a citation here to support your argument?"
- "What events from the book lead you to think this?"

These types of questions cause the learner to think about how to improve the product rather than give the answer.

Another approach is to give specific action items to fix (Barile, 2015). Examples of feedback in this format are as follows.

- "You have three run-on sentences; find them and correct them."

- "You made a claim without evidence. Please provide textual evidence that supports the claim you made."

- "During your conclusion, you added new information. It should only summarize the key points already made. Correct that."

Consider the following practical ideas for providing feedback on student products.

- **Error hunt:** Teachers simply denote the number of errors in a section of text or part of a product without marking specific errors. Students must then locate and correct the errors.

- **Three questions strategy:** Teachers identify a part of the product they want to comment on and write a circled 1 at that point. At the end of the paper or on a separate sheet, they write a question related to that part of the product and leave space below for students to respond. They repeat this process for a second and third question. When students receive their work back, they take ten or fifteen minutes to respond to questions (Wiliam, 2011).

- **Matching strips feedback:** Instead of writing feedback on the product itself, teachers write comments on individual strips of paper. Students receive their products and the comments and must match the comments to the parts of the product (Wiliam, 2011).

Feedback on Performance Assessments

In providing students with feedback about their performance, the use of a rubric—particularly an analytic rubric (see chapter 5, page 87)—offers the opportunity for detailed evaluation, often without the teacher needing to write a lot of descriptive comments. However, we wish to caution teachers against relying too heavily on the rubric alone for student feedback. Although an analytic rubric provides much detail on the specific requirements of the assessment, it will never replace the personal insights a teacher can provide a student. We recommend a combination of rubric scores and written comments to best meet the students' feedback needs on performance assessments.

Feedback on a performance assessment often requires a one-on-one conference. This can usually be timely, since the actual evaluation of the student often takes place during the performance and requires no extended scoring period afterward. Using the rubric as a focal point, teachers go over the feedback to ensure students accurately understand the specifics of the evaluation. Feedback in a one-on-one conference should provide students with the information they need to correct their performance and score higher on the next assessment—information the rubric does not provide. While one-on-one discussions consume instructional time, they are important after an elaborate assessment like a performance assessment.

Informal Assessments as Feedback

Another method for quality feedback is using informal assessments. Some types of informal assessments include the following (Marzano, 2017).

- **Confidence rating techniques:** The teacher asks students to rate their confidence with content using colored cards (green, yellow, red), hand signals (thumbs up, sideways, or down), or technology devices (online surveys, clickers). Teachers can also integrate this strategy into written assessments by asking students to indicate their confidence in the margin next to each answer. For example, students might write + when they feel confident and – or ? when they guessed or feel unsure of their answers. Of course, these confidence ratings do not count against students. They simply provide the teacher with more information about students' knowledge and skills.

- **Response boards:** Students write responses to a question or prompt on individual whiteboards.

- **Unscored assessments:** Students complete assessment items, but the teacher does not score them. The teacher provides the correct answers so students can check their own work.

- **Repeated errors:** The teacher notes a handful of common errors students made on a topic. The teacher reteaches appropriate content or processes and adds assessment items on these past errors to the next assessment. Teachers and students use these items as indicators of more recent understanding—hopefully showing that students have corrected errors in thinking.

- **Assessment corrections:** After getting a scored assessment (typically a pencil-and-paper test) back, students review each item and make a list or chart showing their response to each one and whether it was correct. Then, they analyze any errors, noting whether they were simple mistakes or errors in thinking (and what that misunderstanding was). Finally, they record what they understand better now.

Feedback to Small Groups of Students With Similar Needs

For the sake of efficiency, teachers can give feedback to groups of students with similar needs. For instance, imagine a small group of students in physical education class is struggling with the overhand throw. The teacher would convene the small group of students who need support with this skill and conduct a minilesson. The other students who are already proficient may move into a different activity using the skill of the overhand throw. This saves time for teachers, avoids their needing to repeat the same feedback to multiple students, and prevents wasting the time of students who do not need the feedback. Using common feedback groups helps teachers differentiate instruction to better meet the needs of all students.

Student-to-Student Feedback

In standards-based classrooms, students can give each other feedback. This not only saves the teacher time but can also increase timeliness in feedback to students. Although peer feedback comes with numerous caveats, as we established earlier in the chapter, in a standards-based classroom there are ways for feedback among peers to be effective. Importantly, such peer feedback must be informal in nature: the recipient uses it to improve practice. Teachers should not use peer feedback to assign scores to students. Wiliam (2011) concurred:

> I think it is quite wrong for one student to be placed in the position of evaluating the achievement of another student for the purpose of reporting to parents or others. The purpose of peer assessment should be simply, and purely, to help the individual being assessed improve his work. (p. 137)

Another important caveat is that giving feedback is a skill. As with any other skill, teachers should provide direct instruction before asking students to perform it independently. For instance, Brookhart (2008) provided the following guidelines, which a teacher could share with students.

- Read the response thoroughly. Be certain you understand the response before you give feedback.

- If the teacher provided a rubric or proficiency scale, compare the response to it.

- If the teacher provided samples of other students' work, compare the response to them. See if it is most similar to the exemplar for beginning, proficient, or advanced.

- Keep comments focused on the response itself. Make factual statements like, "You have one example where you need three" or "The introduction doesn't state the purpose." Do not make personal judgments like, "You don't write well" or "Your ideas are silly."

- Support your comments with evidence.

Another suggestion is to teach students to balance positive and critical comments. For example, teachers might set a norm of finding at least two positive elements of the work for every corrective one.

Some teachers elect to have students check with one or more peers prior to seeking direct assistance from the teacher. Other teachers designate particular students as helpers or topic experts who have a clear grasp of the content and the skills to assist others with basic questions. Sometimes this role rotates or changes from unit to unit so many students have the opportunity to participate, though it is imperative that these students have previously demonstrated proficiency on the knowledge and skills in question. As students provide one another feedback, they also learn more.

Student-to-Teacher Feedback

Teachers obtaining feedback from students is important in a standards-based learning environment. About this often-overlooked component of feedback, Hattie (2009) said, "Feedback is most powerful when it comes from the student to the teacher" (p. 173). This is an opportunity for growth and improvement for many educators who have only considered feedback going from the teacher to the student. When students provide feedback about the process of learning and individual tasks, a more collaborative exchange occurs. In turn, the learning environment is one where both the learner and the teacher obtain feedback on a more regular basis. It takes a confident teacher to ask students for honest feedback, even more so to do something with corrective feedback.

Students who have only experienced traditional classrooms may not be naturally inclined to give feedback to the teacher, so teachers should directly ask them. At the beginning of the school year, the teacher could administer a short survey to ascertain students' perceptions about how class is working for them. It may be helpful to seek such feedback again after the first grading period and before the final grading period. Multiple instances of feedback allow teachers to gain insight into what classroom instructional strategies and procedures are working well, what might need some adjustment, and how well they have incorporated students' previous feedback.

The following strategies are helpful for obtaining feedback from students.

- **Exit tickets:** Just prior to leaving class, students answer a question, ask a question, provide an example, or give an explanation about something discussed in class on a slip of paper. The teacher collects them and uses them to adjust instruction the next day.

- **Surveys:** The teacher compiles a brief set of written or online survey questions to ascertain students' understanding of a topic.

- **Dot voting:** This strategy is a means for students to share their opinions about topics or statements. For example, a teacher may ask, "Which of the topics on the board do you need more practice with?" Each student gets three colored sticky dots. They can put all their dots on one topic, or split them among the topics. The teacher quickly sees which topics have the most votes (dots) and works to address the needs accordingly. This strategy is also useful for prioritizing class activities or choices according to student preference. When students see that their vote counts, they are more engaged in their learning.

- **The parking lot:** This tool allows students to share feedback and teachers to monitor learning, respond to needs, and celebrate successes. Hang four large sheets of paper. Title the sheets *pluses* (positive feedback), *deltas* (things that should change), *questions*, and *ideas*. When students have feedback for the teacher, they write it on the appropriate sheet of paper during a break or at the end of class. The teacher monitors the charts and responds to each point as needed. This tool allows students to voice opinions in a positive way, comment, ask questions, request information, or make suggestions without interrupting class.

Planning and Reflecting About Feedback

Teachers in a standards-based learning environment should plan and reflect about feedback. Doing so focuses the classroom climate on learning and helps the teacher improve the skill of giving feedback.

Effective planning includes thinking about which types, formats, and strategies for feedback may be useful during specific instructional cycles. For instance, when might you want to use a parking lot tool to gather students' input? When might an exit ticket work best? As teachers are planning their activities for instruction, they may also want to consider feedback opportunities. It is also helpful to consider when feedback is most useful and warranted. For example, early on in the instructional cycle, the teacher might ask students to share a question they still have in the format of an exit ticket. Teachers might schedule a feedback session at the midpoint of a unit. This is a class period devoted to providing individualized feedback to students or small groups of students. Such a feedback session helps students and teachers reflect and provides time for teachers to modify pacing throughout the unit.

Teachers should regularly reflect about the feedback they provide and how students receive it. The guide in figure 7.2 is an example of how teachers can consider how they typically employ the various components of feedback previously discussed (page 117) and how they might want to improve.

Characteristics	Rationale	Examples	Nonexamples
Specificity	Be sure students know what exactly they did well and did not do well.	"You used three textual examples. Well done!"	"Needs more."
Tone	Be certain my tone is helpful and not overly negative.	"You are getting this! Keep showing your processes."	"What?!"
Timeliness	Be sure to schedule feedback within my instructional cycle so students get feedback promptly and have time to act on it.	Provide weekly feedback for students to use in revising work before a grade is given.	Hand back test scores only after the summative assessment.
Amount	Be sure to give a manageable amount of feedback by focusing on errors rather than small mistakes.	"Here are your three main areas for improvement . . ."	"I highlighted fifty mistakes you made in your paper."
Comparison to Criteria	Be sure to reference the proficiency scale so students can see the criteria throughout the unit.	"I can see from this section that you understand the score 2.0 learning target. To show me score 3.0, you need to . . ."	"Nice work, but you're not all the way there yet. Try again!"

Figure 7.2: Self-reflection on components of feedback.

*Visit **MarzanoResources.com/reproducibles** for a blank reproducible version of this figure.*

Teachers can also reflect on the feedback they give on specific class assignments. Randomly select three pieces of student work with feedback. Review the feedback on those samples through the lenses of specificity, tone, timeliness, amount, and comparison to criteria. Note strengths, as well as which components of quality feedback could improve. Write down what you might do differently in future feedback opportunities. We recommend that collaborative teams engage in this process together. To adapt the process for teams, teachers each bring three samples of student work that they have provided feedback on. The team collaboratively reviews each member's samples, pointing out highly effective feedback and making suggestions for how teammates might improve.

Summary

Feedback is an essential link in the standards-based assessment process. Without it, students will not be able to improve their performance on the standards from one assessment to the next. Teachers can increase the quality of the feedback they give by making sure it is specific, conveyed in a kind but honest tone, timely, limited to a focused amount, and stated in comparison to the criteria on the proficiency scale. As part of the assessment process, teachers should integrate feedback throughout the instructional cycle. We explored strategies for connecting feedback to the proficiency scale, giving feedback on various types of assessments, encouraging students to give feedback to each other and to the teacher, and so on. Feedback in a standards-based classroom should be a truly student-centered process.

Chapter 7 Reflection Questions

1. What are some features of effective feedback?

2. What is one strategy for giving feedback that makes students think?

3. What is the role of student-to-teacher feedback in a standards-based classroom?

4. How can a classroom teacher ensure that feedback fosters improved student performance?

5. Thinking of a unit you have taught or currently teach, how might you apply the concepts or strategies discussed in this chapter?

Epilogue

Assessment is an integral component of standards-based learning. This book is our effort to support classroom teachers in assessing students' progress toward mastery of the standards in a practical way. Without guidance, assessment can feel overwhelming— even daunting—to classroom teachers when considered alongside everything else required for effective teaching. We truly want teachers to feel a high level of confidence regarding high-quality assessment practices that produce meaningful data to inform next steps for instruction. After all, supporting students based on their current levels of performance is the means to higher levels of performance.

The critical assessment topics we addressed in this book demonstrate the interconnected nature of standards-based learning. In the introduction, we reviewed foundational concepts, including priority standards, proficiency scales, and instructional cycles. Chapter 1 explained the roles of assessment in standards-based classrooms: informing student progress and monitoring the effectiveness of instruction. Next, we shared information about assessing the content of proficiency scales at various stages of the instructional cycle through diverse assessment formats in chapter 2. In chapter 3, we explored collaborative practices such as common assessments and data protocols that improve standards-based assessments and teachers' use of assessment to inform instruction. In chapter 4, we provided a detailed examination of the technical quality components of validity, fairness, reliability, and mastery cut scores. Chapter 5 considered how to score assessments in a standards-based classroom. After administering and scoring assessments, teachers must use the resulting information to determine next steps in the learning process, which we discussed in chapter 6. Finally, chapter 7 addressed how to offer effective feedback to learners to ensure they continue moving toward mastery of the standards. In each chapter, we presented key information in practical ways so that classroom teachers feel they can assess learners in a manageable and meaningful way.

Standards-based learning is here to stay. For that reason, it is vital that every classroom teacher gain expertise on how to monitor progress relative to academic standards. Teachers must be able to assess progress in a substantive yet efficient and effective manner. Learners need and deserve the most accurate information teachers can provide regarding their level of learning. It is this accurate information about performance that will inform them about how to improve.

Finally, we encourage all classroom teachers to keep increasing your level of expertise with standards-based learning. Classroom assessments aligned to standards do not have to be the stopping point. Standards-referenced reporting—assigning and reporting grades relative to standards rather than by the traditional 0–100 or A–F metrics—is a logical next step for any educator who is applying the information we share in this book. Once teachers are developing curriculum, designing instruction, delivering lessons, assessing learning, and providing feedback based on standards, it just makes sense to expand the approach to include the way schools communicate grades to students and parents. We look forward to seeing this next step become reality in classrooms everywhere over time. The most accurate information about their performance on the standards is what learners deserve!

References and Resources

Ainsworth, L. (2003). *Power standards: Identifying the standards that matter the most*. Denver, CO: Advanced Learning Press.

American Educational Research Association, American Psychological Association, & National Council on Measurement in Education Joint Committee. (1999). *Standards for educational and psychological testing*. Washington, DC: American Educational Research Association.

American Educational Research Association, American Psychological Association, & National Council on Measurement in Education. (2014). *Standards for educational and psychological testing*. Washington, DC: American Educational Research Association.

Angoff, W. H. (1971). Scales, norms and equivalent scores. In R. L. Thorndike (Ed.), *Educational Measurement* (2nd ed., pp. 508–600). Washington, DC: American Council on Education.

Bailey, K., & Jakicic, C. (2012). *Common formative assessment: A toolkit for Professional Learning Communities at Work*. Bloomington, IN: Solution Tree Press.

Bandalos, D. L. (2004). Can a teacher-led state assessment system work? *Educational Measurement: Issues and Practice, 23*(2), 33–40.

Bangert-Drowns, R. L., Kulik, C. C., Kulik, J. A., & Morgan, M. (1991). The instructional effect of feedback in test-like events. *Review of Educational Research, 61*(2), 213–238.

Barile, N. (2015, January 20). 10 tips for setting successful goals with students. *Education Week*. Accessed at www.edweek.org/tm/articles/2015/01/20/10-tips-for-setting-successful-goals-with.html on August 26, 2022.

Berk, R. A. (1986). A consumer's guide to setting performance standards on criterion-referenced tests. *Review of Educational Research, 56*(1), 137–172.

Berk, R. A. (1995). Something old, something new, something borrowed, a lot to do! *Applied Measurement in Education, 8*(1), 99–109.

Berk, R. A. (1996). Standard setting: The next generation (where few psychometricians have gone before!). *Applied Measurement in Education, 9*(3), 215–235.

Bernhart, V. L. (1998). *Data analysis for comprehensive schoolwide improvement*. Larchmont, NY: Eye on Education.

Bernhart, V. L. (2004). *Data analysis for continuous school improvement* (2nd ed.). Larchmont, NY: Eye on Education.

Bernhart, V. L. (2018). *Data analysis for continuous school improvement* (4th ed.). New York: Routledge.

Bobbit, Z. (2020, February 21). *Split-half reliability: Definition + examples*. Accessed at https://www.statology.org/?s=split+half on January 4, 2022.

Boulet, M., Simard, G., & De Melo, D. (1990). Formative evaluation effects on learning music. *Journal of Educational Research*, *84*(2), 119–125.

Brennen, R. L. (2006). *Educational measurement* (4th ed.). Westport, CT: Praeger.

Brennan, R. L., & Lockwood, R. E. (1980). A comparison of the Nedelsky and Angoff cutting score procedures using generalizability theory. *Applied Psychological Measurement*, *4*(2), 219–240.

Brookhart, S. M. (2008). *How to give effective feedback to your students*. Alexandria, VA: ASCD.

Brookhart, S. M. (2012). Classroom assessment in the context of motivation theory and research. In J. H. McMillan (Ed.), *SAGE handbook of research on classroom assessment* (pp. 35–54). Thousand Oaks, CA: SAGE.

Brookhart, S. M. (2016). *How to create and use rubrics for formative assessment and grading*. Alexandria, VA: ASCD.

Brookhart, S. M. (2017). *How to give effective feedback to your students* (2nd ed.). Alexandria, VA: ASCD.

Brooks, C., Carroll, A., Gillies, R. M., & Hattie, J. A. C. (2019). A matrix of feedback for learning. *Australian Journal of Teacher Education*, *44*(4), 14–32.

Brown, F. G. (1983). *Principles of educational and psychological testing* (3rd ed.). New York: Holt, Rinehart and Winston.

Brown, S. M., & Walberg, H. J. (1993). Motivational effects on test scores of elementary students. *Journal of Educational Researcher*, *86*(3), 133–136.

Buckendahl, C. W., Impara, J. C., & Plake, B. S. (2002, Winter). District accountability without a state assessment: A proposed model. *Educational Measurement: Issues and Practice*, *21*(4), 6–16.

Buckendahl, Plake, B. S., & C. W., Impara, J. C.(2004). A strategy for evaluating district developed assessments for state accountability. *Educational Measurement: Issues and Practice*, *23*(2), 17–25.

Campbell, C. (2013). Research on teacher competency in classroom assessment. In J. H. McMillan (Ed.), *SAGE handbook of research on classroom assessment* (pp. 71–84). Thousand Oaks, CA: SAGE.

Carless, D. (2006). Differing perceptions in the feedback process. *Studies in Higher Education*, *31*(2), 219–233.

Cimbricz, S. (2002). State-mandated testing and teachers' beliefs and practice. *Education Policy Analysis Archives*, *10*(2), 1–14.

Cizek, G. (Ed.). (2012). *Setting performance standards: Foundations, methods, and innovations* (2nd ed.). New York: Routledge.

Cizek, G. J., & Bunch, M. B. (2006). *Standard setting: A guide to establishing and evaluating performance standards on tests*. Thousand Oaks, CA: SAGE.

Collins, J. (2001). *Good to great: Why some companies make the leap and others don't*. New York: HarperCollins.

Colorado Department of Education. (n.d.a). *Performance of Shakespearean material*. Accessed at https://www.cde .state.co.us/sites/default/files/docs/assessmentresourcebank/DramaAndTheatreArts/PerformanceAssessments /Grade8/DTA-PerformanceShakespeareanMaterial-Grade8/DTA-PerformanceShakespeareanMaterial-Grade8 -PerformanceAssessment.doc on December 21, 2021.

Colorado Department of Education. (n.d.b). *Performance of Shakespearean material rubric*. Accessed at https://www.cde .state.co.us/sites/default/files/docs/assessmentresourcebank/DramaAndTheatreArts/PerformanceAssessments /Grade8/DTA-PerformanceShakespeareanMaterial-Grade8/DTA-PerformanceShakespeareanMaterial-Grade8 -Rubric.doc on December 21, 2021.

Colorado Department of Education. (n.d.c). *Sample performance assessment*. Accessed at https://www.cde.state .co.us/sites/default/files/docs/assessmentresourcebank/Math/PerformanceAssessments/Kindergarten/MA -PutItTogetherandTakeItApart-Kindergarten-PerformanceAssessment.pdf on January 21, 2022.

The Commission on Instructionally Supportive Assessment. (2001, October). *Building tests to support instruction and accountability: A guide for policymakers.* Accessed at https://aasa.org/uploadedFiles/Policy_and_Advocacy /files/BuildingTests.pdf on May 12, 2022.

Council of Chief State School Officers. (2018). *Revising the definition of formative assessment.* Washington, DC: Author. Accessed at https://ccsso.org/sites/default/files/2018–06/Revising%20the%20Definition%20of%20 Formative%20Assessment.pdf on May 12, 2022.

DuFour, R., DuFour, R., Eaker, R., Many, T., & Mattos, M. (2016). *Learning by doing: A handbook for Professional Learning Communities at Work.* Bloomington, IN: Solution Tree Press.

DuFour, R., Dufour, R., Eaker, R., Mattos, M., & Muhammad, A. (2021). *Revisiting PLCs at Work* (2nd ed.). Bloomington, IN: Solution Tree Press.

Eaker, R., & Marzano, R. J. (2020). *Professional Learning Communities at Work and High Reliability Schools: Cultures of continuous learning.* Bloomington, IN: Solution Tree Press.

Erickson, F. (2007). Some thoughts on "proximal" formative assessment of student learning. *Yearbook of the National Society for the Study of Education, 106*(1), 186–216.

Feinstein, S. (Ed.). (2006). *The Praeger handbook of learning and the brain.* Westport, CT: Praeger.

Feldt, L. S., & Brennan, R. L. (1993). Reliability. In R. L. Linn (Ed.), *Educational measurement* (3rd ed., pp. 105–146). Phoenix, AZ: Oryx Press.

Ferriter, W. M. (2020). *The big book of tools for collaborative teams in a PLC at Work.* Bloomington, IN: Solution Tree Press.

Fisher, D., & Frey, N. (2007). *Checking for understanding: Formative assessment techniques for your classroom.* Alexandria, VA: ASCD.

Fisher, D., & Frey, N. (2012, September 1). Making time for feedback. *Educational Leadership, 70*(1). Accessed at www.ascd.org/el/articles/making-time-for-feedback on August 26, 2022.

Flett, J. D., & Wallace, J. (2002). Change dilemmas for classroom teachers: Curricular reform at the classroom level. *International Journal for Educational Reform, 11*(4), 309–333.

Flygare, J., Hoegh, J. K., & Heflebower, T. (2022) *Planning and teaching in the standards-based classroom.* Bloomington, IN: Marzano Resources.

Fossey, A. (2013). *Standard setting: Bookmark method overview.* Accessed at https://www.questionmark.com /standard-setting-bookmark-method-overview on December 30, 2021.

Frisbie, D. A. (1988). Reliability of scores from teacher-made tests. *Educational Measurement: Issues and Practice, 7*(1), 25–35.

Frisbie, D. A. (2005). Measurement 101: Some fundamentals revisited. *Educational Measurement: Issues and Practice, 24*(3), 21–28.

Fullan, M. (1991). *The new meaning of educational change.* New York: Teachers College Press.

Fullan, M. (2001). *Leading in a culture of change.* San Francisco: Jossey-Bass.

Fuhrman, S. (2003, September). Redesigning accountability systems for education. *CPRE Policy Briefs.* Philadelphia: University of Pennsylvania.

Gandal, M., & Vranek, J. (2001, September). Standards: Here today, here tomorrow. *Educational Leadership, 59*(1), 6–13.

Gareis, C. R., & Grant, L. W. (2008). *Teacher-made assessments: How to connect curriculum, instruction, and student learning.* New York: Routledge.

Gareis, C. R., & Grant, L. W. (2015). *Teacher-made assessments: How to connect curriculum, instruction, and student learning* (2nd ed.). New York: Routledge.

Gerth, M. (2000). *Ten little ladybugs*. Atlanta, GA: Piggy Toes Press.

Gladwell, M. (2000). *The tipping point: How little things can make a big difference*. Boston: Little, Brown and Company.

Glen, S. (2022a). *Parallel forms reliability (equivalent forms)*. Accessed at www.statisticshowto.com/parallel-forms -reliability on August 24, 2022.

Glen, S. (2022b). *Split-half reliability: Definition, steps*. Accessed at www.statisticshowto.com/split-half-reliability on August 24, 2022.

Glen, S. (2022c). *Test-retest reliability / repeatability*. Accessed at www.statisticshowto.com/test-retest-reliability on August 24, 2022.

Gobble, T., Onuscheck, M., Reibel, A. R., & Twadell, E. (2016). *Proficiency-based assessment: Process, not product*. Bloomington, IN: Solution Tree Press.

Greenberg, J., & Walsh, K. (2012, May). What teacher preparation programs teach about K–12 assessment: A review. Washington, DC: National Council on Teacher Quality. Accessed at https://www.nctq.org/dmsView /What_Teacher_Prep_Programs_Teach_K-12_Assessment_NCTQ_Report on January 20, 2022.

Guskey, T. R. (1994). Making the grade: What benefits students? *Educational Leadership, 52*(2), 14–20.

Guskey, T. R. (Ed.). (1996). *Communicating student learning: 1996 yearbook of the Association for Supervision and Curriculum Development*. Alexandria, VA: ASCD.

Hanover Research. (2014, August). *The impact of formative assessment and learning intentions on student achievement*. Washington, DC: Author. Accessed at https://www.hanoverresearch.com/media/The-Impact-of-Formative- Assessment-and-Learning-Intentions-on-Student-Achievement.pdf on May 12, 2022.

Hanushek, E. A., & Raymond, M. E. (2001). The confusing world of educational accountability. *National Tax Journal, 54*(2), 365–384.

Harsh, J. R. (1974). *The forest, trees, branches and leaves, revisited—Norm, domain, objective and criterion-referenced assessments for educational assessment and evaluation* (Association for Measurement and Evaluation in Guidance monograph no. 1). Fullerton, CA: California Personnel and Guidance Association.

Harvey, J. (2003). The matrix reloaded. *Educational Leadership, 61*(3), 18–21.

Hattie, J. (2009). *Visible learning: A synthesis of over 800 meta-analyses relating to achievement*. New York: Routledge.

Hattie, J. (2012). *Visible learning for teachers: Maximizing impact on learning*. New York: Routledge.

Hattie, J., & Timperley, H. (2007). The power of feedback. *Review of Educational Research, 77*(1), 81–112.

Hattie, J., & Zierer, K. (2019). *Visible learning insights*. New York: Routledge.

Heflebower, T. (2005). *An educator's perception of STARS from selected Nebraska education service unit staff developers* [Unpublished doctoral dissertation]. University of Nebraska–Lincoln.

Heflebower, T. (2009). A seven-module plan to build teacher knowledge of balanced assessment. In T. R. Guskey (Ed.), *The principal as assessment leader* (pp. 93–117). Bloomington, IN: Solution Tree Press.

Heflebower, T., Hoegh, J. K., & Warrick, P. B. (2014). *A school leader's guide to standards-based grading*. Bloomington, IN: Marzano Resources.

Heflebower, T., Hoegh, J. K., & Warrick, P. B. (2017). Get it right the first time! *Kappan, 98*(6), 58–62.

Heflebower, T., Hoegh, J. K., & Warrick, P. B. (2021). *Leading standards-based learning: An implementation guide for schools and districts*. Bloomington, IN: Marzano Resources.

Heflebower, T., Hoegh, J. K., Warrick, P. B., & Flygare, J. (2019). *A teacher's guide to standards-based learning*. Bloomington, IN: Marzano Resources.

Hoegh, J. K. (2020). *A handbook for developing and using proficiency scales in the classroom.* Bloomington, IN: Marzano Resources.

Impara, J. C., & Plake, B. S. (1997). Standard setting: An alternative approach. *Journal of Educational Measurement, 34*(4), 353–366.

Impara, J. C., & Plake, B. S. (1998). Teachers' ability to estimate item difficulty: A test of the assumptions in the Angoff standard setting method. *Journal of Educational Measurement, 35*(1), 69–81.

Kallick, B., & Zmuda, A. (2017). *Students at the center: Personalized learning with habits of mind.* Alexandria, VA: ASCD.

Karantonis, A., & Sireci, S. G. (2006). The bookmark standard-setting method: A literature review. *Educational Measurement: Issues and Practice, 25*(1), 4–12.

Langer, G. M., Colton, A. B., & Goff, L. S. (2003). *Collaborative analysis of student work: Improving teaching and learning.* Alexandria, VA: ASCD.

Lewis, A. C. (1996). Making sense of assessment. *The School Administrator, 53*(11), 8–12.

Linn, R. (2000). Assessments and accountability. *Educational Researcher, 29*(2), 4–16.

Linn, R. (2003, September 19). Task force seeks early end to exam. *Salt Lake Tribune,* p. B3.

Lipton, L., & Wellman, B. (2012). *Got data? Now what? Creating and leading cultures of inquiry.* Bloomington, IN: Solution Tree Press.

Malouff, J. M., Stein, S. J., Bothma, L. N., Coulter, K., & Emmerton, A. J., (2014). Preventing halo bias in grading the work of university students. *Cogent Psychology, 1*(1). Accessed at www.tandfonline.com/doi/full/10.1080/233 11908.2014.988937 on July 19, 2022.

Marzano, R. J. (2003). What works in schools: Translating research into action. Alexandria, VA: ASCD.

Marzano, R. J. (2006). *Classroom assessment and grading that work.* Alexandria, VA: ASCD.

Marzano, R. J. (2010). *Formative assessment and standards-based grading.* Bloomington, IN: Marzano Resources.

Marzano, R. J. (2017). *The new art and science of teaching.* Bloomington, IN: Solution Tree Press.

Marzano, R. J. (2018). *Making classroom assessments reliable and valid.* Bloomington, IN: Solution Tree Press.

Marzano, R. J., & Abbott, S. D. (2022). *Teaching in a competency-based elementary school: The Marzano Academies model.* Bloomington, IN: Marzano Resources.

Marzano, R. J., Dodson, C. W., Simms, J. A., & Wipf, J. P. (2022). *Ethical test preparation in the classroom.* Bloomington, IN: Marzano Resources.

Marzano, R. J., Heflebower, T., Hoegh, J. K., Warrick, P., & Grift, G. (2016). *Collaborative teams that transform schools: The next step in PLCs.* Bloomington, IN: Marzano Resources.

Marzano, R. J. & Kendall, J. S. (1996). *A comprehensive guide to standards-based districts, schools, and classrooms.* Alexandria, VA: ASCD.

Marzano, R. J., & Kendall, J. S. (2007). *The new taxonomy of educational objectives* (2nd ed.). Thousand Oaks, CA: Corwin.

Marzano, R. J., Norford, J. S., Finn, M., & Finn, D., III (2017). *A handbook for personalized competency-based education.* Bloomington, IN: Marzano Resources.

Marzano, R. J., Pickering, D. J., & Pollock, J. E. (2001) *Classroom instruction that works: Research-based strategies for increasing student achievement.* Alexandria VA: ASCD.

Marzano, R. J., Rains, C. L., & Warrick, P. B. (2021). *Improving teacher development and evaluation: A guide for leaders, coaches, and teachers.* Bloomington, IN: Marzano Resources.

Marzano, R. J., & Simms, J. A. (2014). *Questioning sequences in the classroom.* Bloomington, IN: Marzano Resources.

Marzano, R. J., Yanoski, D. C., Hoegh, J. K., & Simms, J. A. (2013). *Using Common Core standards to enhance classroom instruction and assessment.* Bloomington, IN: Marzano Resources.

McTighe, J. (2013). *Core learning: Assessing what matters most.* Provo, UT: School Improvement Network.

McTighe, J., & Ferrara, S. (1998). *Assessing learning in the classroom* (2nd ed.). Washington, DC: National Education Association.

Mills, S. S. (1996). *Classroom assessment format and its potential impact on student learning: Implications for school reform and equal educational opportunity* (Publication No. 9634090) [Doctoral dissertation, University of California, Los Angeles]. ProQuest Dissertations Publishing.

Moss, C. M., & Brookhart, S. M. (2009). *Advancing formative assessment in every classroom: A guide for instructional leaders.* Alexandria, VA: ASCD.

National Assessment of Educational Progress. (2021, November 9). *Score range and percentage of exact agreement for the constructed-response items used in scaling, grade 4 mathematics combined national and state assessment, by item and block: 2015.* Accessed at https://nces.ed.gov/nationsreportcard/tdw/analysis/2015/initial_itemscore_g4math 2015.aspx on September 1, 2022.

National Center for Literacy Education. (2013). *Remodeling literacy learning: Making room for what works.* Champaign, IL: National Council of Teachers of English. Accessed at https://archive.nwp.org/cs/public /download/nwp_file/17664/ncle_report_final.pdf?x-r=pcfile_d on August 23, 2022.

National Governors Association Center for Best Practices & Council of Chief State School Officers. (2010a). *Common Core State Standards for English language arts and literacy in history/social studies, science, and technical subjects.* Washington, DC: Authors. Accessed at www.corestandards.org/assets/CCSSI_ELA%20Standards.pdf on July 12, 2022.

National Governors Association Center for Best Practices & Council of Chief State School Officers. (2010b). *Common Core State Standards for mathematics.* Washington, DC: Authors. Accessed at www.corestandards.org /assets/CCSSI_Math%20Standards.pdf on August 1, 2022.

National Research Council. (2001). *Knowing what students know: The science and design of educational assessment.* Washington, DC: National Academies Press. https://doi.org/10.17226/10019

National School Reform Faculty. (n.d.). *NSRF protocols and activities . . . from A to Z.* Accessed at https://nsrf harmony.org/protocols on August 30, 2022.

Nebraska Department of Education. (2002). *School-based teacher-led assessment and reporting system: A summary.* Lincoln, NE: Author.

Nebraska Department of Education. (2003). *District assessment portfolio.* Lincoln, NE: Author.

Nebraska Department of Education. (2007). *Guidelines and requirements for documenting assessment quality for STARS.* Lincoln, NE: Author.

Neill, M. (2003). High stakes, high risk. *American School Board Journal, 190*(2), 18–21.

Nitko, A. J., & Brookhart, S. M. (2011). *Educational assessment of students* (6th ed.). Boston: Pearson.

Nuthall, G. A. (2005). The cultural myths and realities of classroom teaching and learning: A personal journey. *Teachers College Record, 107*(5), 895–934.

Ohio Department of Education. (2017). *Ohio's learning standards: English language arts.* Accessed at https://education .ohio.gov/getattachment/Topics/Learning-in-Ohio/English-Language-Art/English-Language-Arts-Standards /ELA-Learning-Standards-2017.pdf.aspx?lang=en-US on January 9, 2022.

Ohio Department of Education. (2020). *Physical education.* Accessed at https://education.ohio.gov/Topics/Learning -in-Ohio/Physical-Education on August 24, 2022.

Partnership for 21st Century Learning. (2002). *Learning for the 21st century: A report and MILE guide for 21st century skills*. Accessed at https://files.eric.ed.gov/fulltext/ED480035.pdf on September 1, 2022.

Plake, B. S., & Impara, J. C. (2000). *Technical quality rubric for Nebraska's district performance ratings*. Lincoln, NE: Buros Center for Testing.

Plake, B. S., Impara, J. C., & Buckendahl, C. W. (2004). Technical quality criteria for evaluating district assessment portfolios used in the Nebraska STARS. *Educational Measurement: Issues and Practice, 23*(2), 10–14.

Plake, B. S., Impara, J. C., & Irwin, P. M. (2000). Consistency of Angoff-based predictions of item performance: Evidence of technical quality of results from the Angoff standard setting method. *Journal of Educational Measurement, 37*(4), 347–355.

Popham, W. J. (2002). Right task, wrong tool. *American School Board Journal, 189*(2), 18–22.

Popham, W. J. (2003a). *Test better, teach better: The instructional role of assessment*. Alexandria, VA: ASCD.

Popham, W. J. (2003b). Trouble with testing: Why standards-based assessment doesn't measure up. *American School Board Journal, 190*(2), 14–17.

Popham, W. J. (2006). *Assessment for educational leaders*. Boston: Pearson.

Popham, W. J. (2017). *Classroom assessment: What teachers need to know* (8th ed.). Boston: Pearson.

Ramirez, A. (1999). Assessment-driven reform: The emperor still has no clothes. *Phi Delta Kappan, 81*(3), 204–208.

Reeves, D. (Ed.). (2007). *Ahead of the curve: The power of assessment to transform teaching and learning*. Bloomington, IN: Solution Tree Press.

Reid, J. B. (1991). Training judges to generate standard-setting data. *Educational Measurement: Issues and Practice, 10*(2), 11–14.

Roschewski, P. (2002). *Promising practices, processes, and leadership strategies: Building quality local assessment—An executive summary*. Lincoln: Nebraska Department of Education.

Roschewski, P. (2004). History and background of Nebraska's school-based teacher-led assessment and reporting system (STARS). *Educational Measurement: Issues and Practice, 23*(2), 7–9.

Saphier, J. (2005). *John Adams' promise: How to have good schools for all our children, not just for some*. Acton, MA: Research for Better Teaching.

Selvaraj, A. M., & Azman, H. (2020). Reframing the effectiveness of feedback in improving teaching and learning achievement. *International Journal of Evaluation and Research in Education, 9*(4), 1055–1062.

SHAPE America. (2013). *National physical education standards*. Accessed at www.shapeamerica.org/standards/pe/ on January 31, 2022.

Sirotnik, K. A., & Kimball, K. (1999). Standards for standards-based accountability systems. *Phi Delta Kappan, 81*(3), 209–214.

Steffy, B. E., & English, F. W. (1997). *Curriculum and assessment for world-class schools*. Lancaster, PA: Rowman & Littlefield.

Stiggins, R. J. (1991). Facing the challenges of a new era of educational assessment. *Applied Measurement in Education, 4*(4), 263–273.

Stiggins, R. J. (1995). Professional development: The key to a total quality assessment environment. *NASSP Bulletin, 79*(573), 11–19.

Stiggins, R. J. (2002). Assessment crisis: The absence of assessment *for* learning. *Phi Delta Kappan, 83*(10), 758–765.

Stiggins, R. J., Arter, J., Chappuis, J., & Chappuis, S. (2006). *Classroom assessment for student learning: Doing it right—Using it well*. Portland, OR: Educational Testing Service.

Stiggins, R. J., & Chappuis, J. (2012). *An introduction to student-involved assessment* for *learning* (6th ed.). Boston: Pearson.

Tankersley, K. (2007). *Tests that teach: Using standardized tests to improve instruction.* Alexandria, VA: ASCD.

Thompson, N. (2018, February 23). *What is decision consistency?* Accessed at https://assess.com/what-is-decision -consistency on July 18, 2022.

U.S. Department of Education. (2010). *National Assessment of Educational Progress, 2010 U.S. history assessment.* Accessed at https://mmsdamps.files.wordpress.com/2012/08/history-2-http___nces-ed-gov_nationsreportcard _itmrlsx_backend_questionsummary.pdf on August 23, 2022.

Wagner, T. (2008). *Global achievement gap: Why even our best schools don't teach the new survival skills our children need—And what we can do about it.* New York: Basic Books.

Wiliam, D. (2011). *Embedded formative assessment.* Bloomington, IN: Solution Tree Press.

Wiliam, D. (2018). *Embedded formative assessment* (2nd ed.). Bloomington, IN: Solution Tree Press.

Wisniewski, B., Zierer, K., & Hattie, J. (2020). The power of feedback revisited: A meta-analysis of educational feedback research. *Frontiers in Psychology.* Accessed at https://www.frontiersin.org/articles/10.3389/fpsyg .2019.03087/full on August 30, 2022.

Wolf, K. P. (1993). From informal to informed assessment: Recognizing the role of the classroom teacher. *Journal of Reading, 36*(7), 518–523.

Wyoming Department of Education. (2020). *2020 Wyoming physical education content standards & PLDs.* Accessed at https://edu.wyoming.gov/wp-content/uploads/2020/08/2020-PE-StandardsPLDs_Ed.Input-08.17.20.pdf on August 1, 2022.

Index

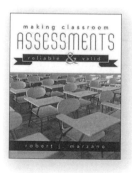
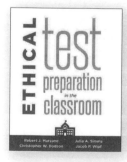